ASSURANCE OF HEAVEN

God's Promise to Anyone Who Believes the Gospel

ASSURANCE OF HEAVEN

God's Promise to Anyone Who Believes the Gospel

GEORGE C. MAINS

XULON PRESS

Xulon Press
2301 Lucien Way #415
Maitland, FL 32751
407.339.4217
www.xulonpress.com

Unless otherwise indicated, Scripture quotations taken from the New King James Version (NKJV). Copyright © 1982 by Thomas Nelson, Inc. Used by permission. All rights reserved.

Scripture quotations taken from the King James Version (KJV)–*public domain.*

Printed in the United States of America.

ISBN-13: 978-1-5456-7109-2

Dedication

This book is dedicated to my sons and daughters-in-law, and to my seven grandchildren; Olivia, Owen, Noah, Eli, Hannah, Micah, and Emma. May this book encourage you to grow in the grace and knowledge of our Lord and Savior Jesus Christ.

Acknowledgments

7 am thankful to my wife of forty-two years, Carol, for her patience with my impatience, and for her continued encouragement and support. "He who finds a good wife finds a good thing, and obtains favor from the Lord" (Prov. 18:22).

I thank my brother in the Lord, Jim Montgomery, for all his help in editing and encouragement.

I would also like to thank many of my brothers in the Lord for all the godly conversations over the years. This book is a compilation of all those discussions. "As iron sharpens iron, so a man sharpens the countenance of his friend" (Prov. 27:17).

Most importantly, I thank the Lord Jesus Christ for saving a wretch like me.

Contents

Introduction

----------❯○◦❮○----------

*D*o you lack assurance of salvation? Are you one hundred percent sure you will go to heaven?

Many believers do not have this assurance for a number of reasons. Some begin to doubt God's word after they are saved. Others may be ignorant of their position as a child of God, due to a lack of personal study. Many begin to question their salvation because they are subtly taught to look at their performance. Often teachers confuse passages that speak to Christian living (walking by faith) with those that address deliverance from sin's penalty (hell).

Today you can listen to a variety of teachers on radio and television. Some stations broadcast Christian teaching around the clock. The internet adds to this dimension of Christian broadcasting, also. But because a person is popular doesn't mean that all of their teachings are correct. Most of those who preach via modern day media do so because they are financed by people who agree with their doctrine. Study Bibles and commentaries add to the confusion as well. These things deceived me for a time along the way.

If you are not grounded in the gospel, you may be misled. Wrong teaching concerning the gospel will cause you to lack assurance of heaven; something that God wants you to have. There are those who teach you can lose your salvation. Others believe baptism is necessary. Still, others think religious sacraments are needed to get to heaven. Confusion about salvation abounds in the church, and it usually affects most everyone at some point. Many teach that you won't go to heaven if you don't persevere. I bought into that without even realizing what it meant. In addition, you may be told that a "true" believer will produce good works and be committed to serving the Lord. All this stuff made me doubt. Had I done enough? Was I good enough? Eventually, I realized there was something askew.

That something askew would take a couple of years to untangle. Like a jumbled bunch of fishing line, it takes time to unravel incorrect spiritual beliefs—things like predestination, carnality, fellowship with God, good works, and repentance. In the process, I would learn about the three tenses of salvation, the power, and deception of the sin nature remaining in the child of God, and how many spiritual leaders blend sanctification and justification truths. It's disheartening to me now to hear how many people create spiritual fogginess about salvation by adding requirements to it.

This book comes from my own personal spiritual misunderstandings, pitfalls, and experiences. Some of it came from my own doings, and some from listening to the wrong people. The Bible says you can know you have everlasting life (1 John 5:13). Believing the right gospel should give you assurance. But many who profess to know Jesus do not know for sure. Often they do not have assurance, because they are subtly taught a performance-based salvation. If you judge your salvation upon your personal goodness and what you do, you will never know for certain that you will go to heaven.

This book will help you look at what you believe concerning assurance and evaluate it by Scripture, so that you can begin to live an abundant life, knowing that as a child of God, you are completely forgiven and restored. Heaven is sure for anyone in Christ. God's not going to zap you when you do something wrong. That's the way I used to think. That's why understanding the gospel correctly is absolutely necessary for eternal life, living a life pleasing to God, and that is good for you.

I hope this book will answer some questions about Christian teaching today and why it often adds more uncertainty to salvation than helping. From my perspective and experience in church leadership, I have found that many believers do not understand their position in Christ. They look at themselves for assurance, rather than looking to Him. If you struggle with assurance, it may well be due to your misunderstanding of the character of God and your position as one of His children. You subtly may have been taught a performance-driven gospel.

For me, clarity began slowly when I started to read and study the Bible. And more clarity came by understanding from the Bible that the gospel is absolutely free to anyone. Faith in Jesus plus nothing equals everything. Right before Jesus died, He said, "It is finished" (John 19:29). I learned to trust what God said. I quit listening to those who confused the good news. My assurance came when I stopped looking at myself, and in faith looked to Jesus and His promises. Trusting His promise of everlasting life, by faith alone in Christ alone, is the only solution to erasing doubts. Jesus said, "Most assuredly, I say to you, he who believes in Me has everlasting life" (John 6:47). It really is that simple.

Chapter 1

The B-I-B-L-E

———⟶○⟿⟿○⟵———

"The B-I-B-L-E, yes, that's the book for me." That was a song I sang in Sunday school as a youngster. Like the song, "Jesus Loves Me", the lyrics have been stuck in my mind for over sixty years. But it hadn't been the book for me. I hadn't read any of it for almost a decade as a young man. For at least three to four of those years in my mid-twenties, I had this ongoing nagging thought: *I need to read the Bible.* I didn't ignore that still small voice, but I kept putting it off. Thankfully, it never went away.

So eventually I picked it up and began to read some. It surely couldn't hurt. Nothing major changed initially. It was a slow process over time, but my desire grew more and more to know what God said. The Bible is a big book that is made up of sixty-six books written by forty authors over a period of fifteen hundred years to different groups of people with much harmony and continuity. It takes a lot of time and effort to put things into their proper context. However, I began to realize if I wanted to know God and what He expected of me, then I needed to know His Word.

This is a huge hindrance in the spiritual development of the church. Most Christians do not read and study the Bible as a relational skill, in order to know God. I didn't for a number of years, and it was detrimental to what I believed and the way I lived. I know firsthand, that apart from knowing the truth of God's Word,

1

one cannot begin to know Him in a personal way. Many will sit and listen to a sermon and think they have done their religious duty for the week. But that would be like spending an hour a week with your wife expecting to have an intimate, growing personal relationship. Not possible!

Secondly, failing to understand the Bible in its proper context is another hindrance in growing and having assurance. Most of the New Testament books are written to churches, to the saints. Saints are simply believers. It is the instruction book for those who have trusted in Christ as Savior. Most of it is written for the purpose of learning how to grow as a child of God.

Sure, there are verses in those letters about deliverance from the penalty of sin, justification. There is also much about our position in Christ as a child of God. But there is also much about how to live as a child of God, to live a life that is consistent with our position. There are warnings to believers not to fall away. There are exhortations to believers to persevere in trials and tribulations. There are instructions to believers not to live like the unbelieving world. However, believers are never told to judge their salvation according to their behavior. Learned men teach that you can judge a person's salvation based upon their conduct. The Bible doesn't.

That's why listening only to a man or woman for truth can also be detrimental. People get biblical truth wrong all the time. Some leaders and teachers are ignorant. Some do it for personal gain. Some may do it as merely a way to make a living. Sometimes it is an honest mistake. Whatever the reason, never simply believe what the preacher or teacher tells you about the Bible, including the writer of this book. No human gets it all right. We all have wrongly interpreted the Bible because we're human and we make mistakes. But making mistakes in main and essential areas of understanding the Bible can have a significant impact on life and even for eternity.

I know that a lot of people think you have to have a seminary degree to preach or teach the Bible. But when you examine commentaries written by educated men, you soon discover there is a considerable amount of disagreement even in some significant areas of doctrine. And think about it for a second. Were the apostles educated men? When Peter and John came before the Sanhedrin, they marveled "when they saw the boldness of Peter and John, and perceived that they were uneducated and untrained men ... And they realized that they had been with Jesus" (Acts 4:13). They didn't have degrees. They were just faithful and teachable, and they had been with Jesus.

I'm not trying to demean seminary education. But there are many seminaries, and they teach different things. You can always find a school that agrees with you. I am trying to demonstrate that when it comes to humans, no matter how educated and sincere, they do not agree with one another. You must be a Berean if you do not want to be misled in the truth. The people in Berea checked out what the apostle Paul was teaching. They "searched the Scriptures daily to find out whether these things were so" (Acts 17:11). And so should you. It's for your own spiritual well-being.

Over the years, a number of people attending adult studies that I led would generally prepare by reading the notes of a popular study Bible beforehand. I had the same study Bible and was myself misled to a degree by that same commentary several years before this. That's why I am advocating the things in this chapter. During class, often one would express that writer's view, which was in total opposition to my newer understanding of the subject. I tried to help them see their error by encouraging them to read opposing viewpoints, and most importantly, to learn what the overarching teaching of the entire Scriptures is on any given subject. The words of commentaries are the words of men. And just because someone has three or four degrees doesn't make him right.

Being teachable is so significant when it comes to growing in your relationship with God. It requires humility no matter who you are. The purpose of reading and understanding Scripture is not to gain knowledge. Knowledge puffs up. For sure it requires knowing things. But the purpose of knowing is so you can apply those truths in your life. The study of God's Word is to know Him. It's a relational skill that we should develop as we go through life. It's not about winning an argument about some doctrinal issue. His Word should be "a lamp unto my feet and a light unto my path" (Ps. 119:105). If we trust in Him, He will guide us according to His Word. "Trust in the Lord with all your heart, and lean not on your own understanding; in all your ways acknowledge Him, and He shall direct your paths" (Prov. 3:5,-6). Job treasured the Word of God more than his necessary food (Job 23:12). That should be our attitude when it comes to the Bible.

For those who are parents, you want to see your children grow up to be responsible adults. The Lord wants the same thing for us as well. God wants us to grow up spiritually, to become mature in the faith. Reading, meditating, and studying God's Word with the eyes of faith is the only avenue to achieve this. Jesus said "man shall not live by bread alone, but by every word that proceeds from the mouth of God" (Matt. 4:4). That's how important His Word is in our walk of faith. Knowing His Word is knowing Him. The two cannot be separated.

Many people pray; most of the world prays. But if your prayer is not directed to the God of the Bible, it is at best just speaking into the air. Those prayers are being offered up to a god devised in the mind of man. And for those who know the Lord, praying alone is merely a one-sided conversation. Have you ever talked with someone or instead listened to someone in a one-sided conversation? Not much of a relationship can be built in a one-way conversation. We need to hear from God. That's our greatest need.

God gave us the Bible to train us. "All Scripture is given by inspiration of God, and is profitable for doctrine, for reproof, for correction, for instruction in righteousness that the man of God may be complete, thoroughly equipped for every good work" (2

4

Tim. 3:16-17). Apart from God's Word, it would be impossible to grow up as a mature believer. His Word even instructs us how to pray and what we should ask for. So how would it be possible for anyone to know what the Lord expects of us if we are not getting to know Him through His Word?

Nevertheless, educated men and women distort the truths of Scripture. Some of those distortions are serious in nature. If you have understood the gospel and have trusted the Lord Jesus Christ to save you, but lack assurance, your insecurity might be coming from wrong teaching about the grace of God. Recently, I heard a preacher on a popular Christian radio station promote such a view. This pastor affirmed that baptism was not necessary for salvation. But then turned around and said if you didn't have faith to be baptized, then you didn't have faith to save you. That is called double-speak. It's making two statements that contradict one another. This kind of mist in the pulpit will create a fog in the pew.

The fog is even more substantial when we fail to realize Satan knows God's Word and he misuses it and perverts it. He distorted it when he spoke to Eve (Gen. 3:4). He also misrepresented it when he spoke with Jesus (Matt. 4). He can take people captive to do his will, even believers (2 Tim. 2:26). There is spiritual warfare in this life that most believers give little credence. It plays out in human affairs, especially when we fail to rightly divide the Word.

So a lack of assurance may begin by failing to know God's Word and applying it correctly. If you are not engaging with God regularly, you will be easily deceived into believing a spiritual lie. And a lie just may be whispered in your ear, "You're too bad. God will never accept you. Look at what you did." Or some teacher may lead you to believe that you haven't done enough to earn God's favor. All of that is spiritual warfare, and it can't be dealt with apart from faith in God and His Word. Jesus said, "Most assuredly, he who believes in Me has everlasting life" (John 6:47). Getting to heaven does not depend on you. Don't doubt God's Word. Believe it! If you are looking for assurance, take God at His word.

Chapter 2

The Influence of Spiritual Warfare

───────○◁◅◦◦▷▷○─────────

I am always amazed when I read the results of a survey of Christians and the percentage who do not believe in a literal devil. The Bible is clear that he is real and "walks about like a roaring lion, seeking whom he may devour" (1 Pet. 5:8). The whole world lies under his influence (1 John 5:19). Jesus described him as a murderer from the beginning and that he is the father of lies (John 8:44). However, he is crafty for he transforms himself into an angel of light (2 Cor. 11:14)! Jesus rebuked Peter for siding with Satan when Peter expressed opposition to the will of God (Matt. 16:23). Most people think of him as the caricature with horns, a tail, and a pitchfork. But in reality, he is way more deceptive than that. The good-looking guy with the three-piece suit in the pulpit could well be representing him (2 Cor. 11:13-15).

Because he is in rebellion against God, his purpose can be understood at least in two ways. First, he works in people to blind their minds to the gospel so that they do not get saved (2 Cor. 4:4). And secondly, he has created the world system to appeal to the old nature; the lust of the flesh, the lust of the eyes, and the pride of life (1 John 2:16). He designed it to distract unbelievers away from the Lord, and attempts to derail believers from their intended purpose so that they become unfaithful and unfruitful as a result (Matt. 13:21-22). Everybody is subject to his influence.

The Bible is plain. The devil blinds the minds of the unbelieving. But how does he do it? He uses people. The language of God is truth. God does not speak any lies. The lies come from the evil one. "He is a liar and the father of it" (John 8:44). When we lie, we are siding with him. Satan takes people captive to do his will, knowingly or unknowingly (2 Tim. 2:26). And if you are taken captive to do his will, you are living or promoting a lie.

But spiritual warfare does not only involve the devil and his workers; it involves you and me. Every one of us has a fallen nature, a sin nature. We are born with this, and the devil works in conjunction with our fallen nature. The Bible describes our nature straightforwardly, honestly, and truthfully: "The heart is deceitful above all things and desperately wicked" (Jer. 17:9). The heart is the inner control center of man involving the mind, will, and emotions. The result of a deceitful heart is, "there is not a just man on earth who does good and does not sin" (Eccles. 7:20).

The devil appeals to our old nature through the world system to influence our emotions. He wants our emotions to persuade our mind to affect change in our will. But God works in the opposite way. He wants to influence our mind through His Word to affect change in our will, and our emotions will follow. Think of it this way. The mind is the engine, the will is the coal car following, and the caboose is the emotion at the end of the train.

For example, let's say you have been mistreated. You have been wrongly passed over for a job. The local school district hired the daughter-in-law of the school board president. She just graduated from college and has no experience teaching. You have previously taught a year and substituted faithfully for eight years in the district. You respond in anger and slander both the person and the school board. In resentment, you quit working for that school. The caboose (emotions) is driving the train at that moment. Emotions easily lead humans. But God wants to lead us according to His Word. In this case, "Do not be overcome by evil, but overcome evil with good" (Rom. 12:21).

This combination of realities about the devil and us can lead to disastrous consequences if we are unaware of these truths from God's Word, the Bible. Most Christians do not respect his power in the world system to influence us. But the apostle Paul was aware of his influence when he wrote to the Ephesian church: "Put on the whole armor of God that you be able to stand against the wiles of the devil. For we do not wrestle with flesh and blood, but against principalities, against powers, against the rulers of the darkness of this age, against spiritual hosts of wickedness in the heavenly places" (Eph. 6:1-12).

We see our struggle with people and circumstances of life. But the real battle is going on behind the scenes and affecting the minds of people.

Back in the 1960s, Paul Harvey, a popular national radio commentator on the news, in his unique style, aired a famous commentary titled, "If I were the Devil." Following is an excerpt:

> If I were the devil ... I would gain control of the most powerful nation in the world ... I would delude their minds into thinking that they had come from man's effort, instead of God's blessings ... I would promote an attitude of loving things and using people, instead of the other way around ... I would dupe entire states into relying on gambling for their state revenue ... I would convince people that character is not an issue when it comes to leadership ... I would make it legal to take the life of unborn babies.[1]

---

[1] David Mikkelson, "Paul Harvey: 'If I Were the Devil' Did radio commentator Paul Harvey pen an essay entitled 'If I Were the Devil'?" October 25, 2004. https://www.snopes.com/fact-check/if-i-were-the-devil/.

His observations were prophetic. If you were to read the whole thing with its updated versions, he saw things in his day years before they would spill out nationwide. He understood the scheme of the devil. There is only one major thing I believe he failed to include. If I were the devil, I would try to confuse and change the most important message: the gospel. If he could confuse the message, if he could muddle it up, if he could slightly alter it, then he could affect the eternal destiny of people in an attempt to thwart the plan of God. We will see how that is playing out in the church today.

The World's Way vs. God's Way

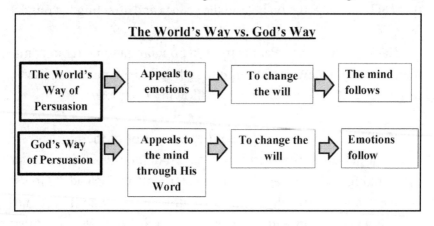

Chapter 3

The Gospel: What is it?

———∘◦⟨≫≫∘⟩◦———

I have been in church leadership serving as a deacon and elder for over three decades. The church that I serve in now has been making diligent attempts to reach people with the gospel in our community and to make disciples, the very things that Jesus instructed His disciples to do (Matt. 28:19; Mark 16:15). His disciples were to teach others to "observe all the things" that Jesus commanded them (Matt. 28:20). Obviously, two of those things the disciples would have taught others would be to preach the gospel and make disciples. Every succeeding generation would be commanded to do the same. That's the method God has designed to reach people.

In our outreach attempts, we try to build relationships with people at festivals, fairs, parades, martial art ministries, dance ministries, and a variety of other things from time to time. What I found out early on participating in some of these events and talking to hundreds of people is that most have no clue how to begin a relationship with God. Even many Christians lack assurance of their eternal destination. Why? In almost every case the person is hoping in their own personal goodness to get them there. In other words, they are hoping that the good things they do will outweigh the bad things.

All unbelievers get saved by believing in Christ alone for salvation. Then as they begin their walk, sometimes a misunderstanding of the gospel begins to influence them. They think that they have to be good, at least outwardly, to maintain it or to keep it. Their thinking is often reinforced through pastors and teachers who also do not understand grace and fail to rightly divide the word. I'm not saying we should abuse the grace of God. What I am saying is that the more one understands His grace, the more likely that person will want to grow spiritually for the proper reason.

Understanding grace promotes godliness, not legalism. To me, legalism is a desire to please God or gain His favor by performance rather than by faith. Because of sin, we are all wired to think this way. But only by faith can you please God (Heb. 11:6). Faith is positively responding to God's word. His love compels us that we should live for Him because He died for us (2 Cor. 5:14-15). That is the primary motivation for the Christian life.

Furthermore, most of us are taught from the time we are a toddler, if you are good, you will be praised. If you do well in school, you may be rewarded with a scholarship. If you work hard in your career, you will get a raise and may be promoted. Everything we know is based upon our performing, our doing the right things to receive the reward. We carry the same thinking over into our concept of God. We have devised our own God if we think we can be restored to a relationship with Him by trying to be good enough. No one deserves to go to heaven, and no one can be good enough to get there. Many add to this confusion by frontloading or backloading the gospel. For now, let's make sure we understand the gospel. What is it? The Bible defines it in 1 Corinthians 15:1-4: "Moreover brethren I delivered to you the gospel... For I delivered to you first of all that which I also received: that Christ died for our sins according to the Scriptures and that He was buried, and that He rose again the third day according to the Scriptures."

The apostle Paul reminded the church at Corinth that the first thing he shared with them was the gospel. He writes this to them because of the influence of some who were saying there is no resurrection of the dead. His point was that if there is no resurrection for believers, then Christ is not risen and their (our) faith is futile (1 Cor. 15:12-13).

"But Christ is risen from the dead" (1 Cor. 15:20). Therefore, all believers have the assurance of a resurrected body (1 Cor. 15:22).

The truth is that the gospel is simple. Jesus Christ, fully God and fully man, died to pay the penalty for our sins. He died in our place. He was our sufficient substitute. They buried Him in a tomb and on the third day He rose from the dead, proving that He has the power over sin and death. After His resurrection, He was seen alive by five hundred people (1 Cor. 15:5-9).

Man's only response to be saved from eternal punishment in the Lake of Fire is to believe in Him. "But as many as received Him, to them He gave the right to become children of God, to those who believe in His name" (John 1:12). The word "believe" in the Bible means to be persuaded of, to put confidence in.[2] Believing is a faith response. It requires that an individual understands his need for a savior. Everyone is guilty. "All have sinned and fall short of the glory of God" (Rom. 3:23). "All" has serious implications for the human race. Each person is a condemned sinner, helpless to restore one's relationship with God because He is holy and we are not.

"To believe in His name" means to accept the truth about His identity and His history. His identity is that He came to Earth fully human and fully God. He is the Son of God, and He is the Son of Man. His history is that He died a substitutionary death for the sins of the world and rose again bodily on the third day. When you believe in His name, you believe this about Jesus.

---

[2] W.E. Vine, Merrill F. Unger, William White Jr. Vine's Complete Expository Dictionary of Old and New Testament Words (Nashville, Camden, New York: Thomas Nelson Publishers, 1985), 61 [New Testament].

So when a sinner understands his or her dilemma of perishing, understands who Jesus is and what He did, and believes in Him, then that person is immediately saved from eternal punishment. Not only rescued from the Lake of Fire, but also restored to a relationship with God. Nothing can snatch you out of His hand, and you shall never perish (John 10:28). That is God's promise to whoever believes in Jesus for everlasting life and forgiveness of sins (John 6:47; Eph. 1:7).

At the moment of faith in Jesus, the Bible tells us that a person is justified by faith. "Man is not justified by the works of the law but by faith in Jesus Christ" (Gal. 2:16). "For all have sinned and fall short of the glory of God, being freely justified by His grace through the redemption that is in Jesus Christ" (Rom. 3:23-24). Justification is the act whereby our legal standing has changed. A guilty sinner is now declared righteous in his standing with God. The perfect righteousness of Christ is credited to the believing sinner (2 Cor. 5:21).

Salvation is not a work of man. It is a work of God. God did everything necessary for man to be restored to fellowship with Him. The only requirement of an individual is to believe. And the Bible states that to believe is not a work on man's part. "But to him who *does not work, but believes* on Him who justifies the ungodly, his faith is accounted for righteousness" (Rom. 4:5, emphasis mine). This verse clearly contrasts believing from works. A lost man or woman will never get saved by trying to work for it.

Secondly, it should also be noted that salvation is the gift of God. "For by grace you have been saved through faith and that not of yourselves; *it is the gift of God*, not of works, lest anyone should boast" (Eph. 2:8-9, emphasis mine). Look closely at what this verse is saying: "For by grace you have been saved [past tense moment of time] through faith [the way one receives the gift], and that not of yourselves [nothing one does]; it is the gift of God [a gift requires nothing of the recipient other than accepting the gift]; not of works [turning from sin; reforming oneself; doing good things; not doing

14

bad things; communion; baptism; etc.], <u>lest anyone should boast</u> [One could brag if it required works] (Eph. 2:8-9, emphasis mine).

The very definition of a gift means there are no strings attached. There is no requirement to meet. For example, let's say I give you a watch and tell you that you have to wear it to church on Sundays. And if you don't, then I am going to take it back. That would not qualify as a gift. It would be an exchange. I give you a watch, and you keep it if you faithfully wear it on Sundays. However, a gift has no qualifiers. You get to choose how you will use it. In the case of the watch, you decide how to use it and when to wear it. When it comes to the gift of salvation, you get to make daily choices about how you respond to the giver of the gift. He doesn't take it away if you do not respond appropriately.

And finally, when a gift is offered, it is only complete when the recipient accepts it. That's what one does in regards to the gift of salvation. An individual receives the benefit of forgiveness and everlasting life by believing in what the Lord did for sinners, not by working for it. At the moment of faith in Christ as Savior, a condemned sinner passes from eternal death to eternal life.

God made it simple. It took one act of disobedience to plunge the entire human race into sin. Sinners only beget sinners. It's in our DNA, so to speak, passed down from Adam. People wonder why the world is like it is. It's because of sin. But God offers us a pardon purchased by Him at great cost through His Son, the Lord Jesus Christ. Any individual can receive the gift and be restored to a relationship with God by one decision to believe the gospel. That is where assurance should be: in the Lord Jesus Christ.

Have you received the gift of everlasting life by faith alone in Jesus Christ alone? If you haven't, you can do so right now by agreeing with God that you are a condemned sinner helpless to save yourself. And then believe on the Lord Jesus Christ to save you. "Believe on the Lord Jesus Christ and you will be saved" (Acts 16:31).

Salvation from the Penalty of Sin (Justification)
The Problem

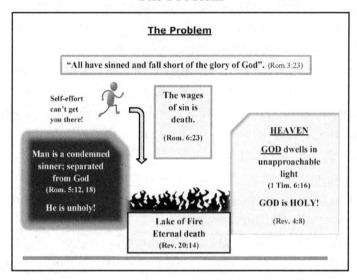

The Problem

"All have sinned and fall short of the glory of God". (Rom.3:23)

Self-effort can't get you there!

The wages of sin is death.
(Rom. 6:23)

Man is a condemned sinner; separated from God
(Rom. 5:12, 18)

He is unholy!

HEAVEN

GOD dwells in unapproachable light
(1 Tim. 6:16)

GOD is HOLY!
(Rev. 4:8)

Lake of Fire
Eternal death
(Rev. 20:14)

The Solution

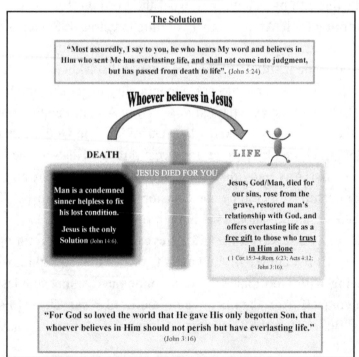

The Solution

"Most assuredly, I say to you, he who hears My word and believes in Him who sent Me has everlasting life, and shall not come into judgment, but has passed from death to life". (John 5:24)

Whoever believes in Jesus

DEATH

LIFE

JESUS DIED FOR YOU

Man is a condemned sinner helpless to fix his lost condition.

Jesus is the only Solution (John 14:6).

Jesus, God/Man, died for our sins, rose from the grave, restored man's relationship with God, and offers everlasting life as a free gift to those who trust in Him alone
(1 Cor.15:3-4;Rom. 6:23; Acts 4:12; John 3:16).

"For God so loved the world that He gave His only begotten Son, that whoever believes in Him should not perish but have everlasting life." (John 3:16)

Chapter 4

Understanding the Three Tenses of Salvation

———————◦⚜◦———————

I was a Christian for twenty years before I began to realize the Bible taught not only that a believer has been saved but is also being saved and one day will be saved. This spiritual truth surfaced after I began to read and study the Bible. Salvation is not only a past event; it is also a present experience and will be one day a final and completed deliverance. It was several years after this that I understood it in the following way: that a believer has been delivered from the penalty of sin, is being delivered from the power of sin, and one day will be delivered from the presence of sin. The penalty, power, and presence of sin parallel the biblical terminology of justification, sanctification, and glorification.

There are many Christians that have been raised in churches that have two chairs theology (more about this in Chapter 8). You are either saved or unsaved. I remember when I was baptized as an outward profession of my faith in Jesus Christ, the church greeted me along with the others who were baptized that day. Since I was a young man, I had the impression that I had arrived. I was going to heaven. But I failed to understand that the gift of everlasting life begins at the moment of faith. You don't have to wait to die to get it. I also didn't realize salvation from the penalty of sin is only the beginning of the race, not the end of the race. And I believe many evangelical churches have given that impression to a lot of new believers over the years. Because of it, these churches as a whole have failed to make disciples. This failure has produced numbers of believers who lack good biblical understanding, do not grow to spiritual maturity, and lack assurance of their salvation.

Why does it matter? It matters for a number of reasons. First of all, God wants to deliver us from the power of sin so we can live a productive spiritual life that glorifies Him and is good for us. So if one is unaware of this theological truth, how would it be possible to grow and to glorify God?

Secondly, it is significant to understand Scripture correctly, so one does not become confused and is not taken captive by poor teaching, causing fear and doubt. For example, the word "save" or "saved" doesn't always mean to be delivered from sin's penalty, which is eternal death. Sometimes the Bible uses it about a child of God being saved from the power of sin. Sometimes it is used of someone being saved from a dangerous situation. It's not always a reference to being saved from hell. But if you have a theology that doesn't allow for a third chair, then you almost always see it in reference to salvation from hell. But sometimes that is not the case.

Vine's Expository Dictionary of Old and New Testament Words defines "save" as follows:

A. Of material and temporal deliverance from danger, suffering, etc.
B. Of the spiritual and eternal salvation granted immediately by God to those who believe on the Lord Jesus Christ.
C. Of the present experiences of God's power to deliver from the bondage of sin...

D. Of the future deliverance of believers at the second coming of Christ...[3]

Vines reveals in the definition of "save" a total of eight variations of meaning for it in the New Testament. We will look only at these four to understand the variety of meaning the word can carry from the context. And remember most importantly that the context of a word in a sentence, in a paragraph, and a book defines the meaning. It's no different in the Bible.

For example, if I ask you what the word "trunk" means, what would you say? You might say an elephant trunk, the trunk of a car, a tree trunk, the midsection of the body, or a storage chest. However, you can only guess what I mean until I use it in a sentence. So if I ask you to help me get the groceries out of the trunk after I had just come home from the store, you immediately would know what I meant. That's the way God has wired our brains to understand language.

In the first usage of "save", you see the word means to deliver from danger. "Then his disciples came to Him and awoke Him, saying, 'Lord save us! We are perishing!'" (Matt. 8:25). If we didn't read the context, one could argue His disciples asked Jesus to save them from hell. But in the context you understand they had gotten into a boat with Jesus and a great storm kicked up, and they thought they would physically die. They asked Him to save them from physical danger.

The second meaning is one that we often give to the word, to be saved from hell (eternal salvation). "For this is good and acceptable in the sight of God our Savior, who desires all men to be saved and come to the knowledge of the truth" (1 Tim. 2:4). It's apparent from the context that it is talking about sinners being delivered from the penalty of sin, eternal separation from God. It's speaking of eternal salvation.

---

[3] Vine. Complete Expository Dictionary, 61 [New Testament].

The third definition is usually more difficult to detect and often is confused with the second definition. God's desire is not only to save believers from the penalty of sin, but also the bondage of sin, or the power of sin. James wrote to believers, urging them to "lay aside all filthiness and overflow of wickedness and receive with meekness the implanted word, which is able to save your soul" (James 1:21).

In 1:18, James indicates they were saved already from the penalty of sin: "Of His own will He brought us forth by the word of truth that we [James and the recipients of the letter] might be a kind of firstfruits of His creatures." In verse 19, he refers to them as "beloved brethren," a reference to their spiritual relationship.

However, like the Corinthian church, they had a variety of issues in regards to the faith. They were double-minded (1:8). They were not doers of the word (1:22). They showed partiality to the richer brethren (2:3-4). They fought and warred among themselves (4:2). They prayed for the wrong things (4:3). He called them adulterers, meaning they committed spiritual adultery by becoming a friend of the world (4:4). They did not allow the Spirit of God through the Word of God to deliver them from the power of sin. If they received the implanted word, it would save their souls.

The word "soul" can refer to one's physical life. It's not used here in the sense of the body being separated from the soul at death. In other words, more Holy Spirit-led obedient living would save them at that moment from the bondage of sin, which usually causes a variety of distresses. Sinful living causes separation in fellowship with other believers. More significantly, it causes a separation in fellowship with the Lord so that his hand of blessing will not be on the sinner. King David experienced this loss of fellowship and even the degradation of his physical well-being before confessing his sin (Ps. 32:3-5). That's how living sinfully can affect us.

So it's vital that we understand "save" in its proper context when it means to be delivered from the power of sin. If we don't, it will lead to a misunderstanding of the grace of God. It will also underestimate the capabilities of the old nature in a believer, causing one to be unfruitful and useless. And it can distort the gospel by adding good works to it.

The fourth definition of "save" is in reference to the deliverance of believers at the second coming of Christ or when we go to be with Him at physical death. It is the deliverance from the presence of sin. "And do this, knowing the time, that now it is high time to awake out of sleep; for our salvation is nearer than when we first believed" (Rom. 13:11). This is a reference to the believer's deliverance from the presence of sin either at the return of Christ or at the believer's death prior to Christ coming for the church.

If one has believed in Jesus as Savior and is not being delivered from the power of sin, there is no sanctification occurring in one's life. The child of God is useless and unfruitful (2 Pet. 1:9). Such a person is delivered from the penalty of sin the moment he trusts in Christ as Savior. He is guaranteed to be delivered from the presence of sin as well because it is based on God's faithfulness, not on man's faithfulness. "If we [the apostle Paul writing to Timothy] are faithless, He remains faithful; He cannot deny Himself" (2 Tim. 2:13). But nothing good can happen for the child of God who is living in such a way.

There are consequences for sin, and some of them can be significant. "Do not be deceived, God is not mocked; for whatever a man sows, that he shall reap. For he who sows to the flesh will of the flesh reap corruption, but he who sows to the Spirit will reap of the Spirit everlasting life" (Gal. 6:7-8). Certainly, the apostle is not saying everlasting life is earned by reaping. He is writing to believers to warn them that sowing to the flesh can lead to a ruined life. In comparison, sowing to the Spirit will reap in their physical life a quality that God calls everlasting life. For only in the Spirit can a believer realize that quality of life whereby he can be useful and fruitful to the Lord.

It is only in this life that we have the opportunity to be faithful, fulfilling God's purpose to serve Him. To be delivered from the power of sin, a believer must learn to surrender in the moments of time and the situations of life by faith. It requires trusting God and His Word, depending on His power to give us the strength and ability to carry out His will, not my will. How does one love your enemy? Apart from the Lord, we can't.

Being delivered from the penalty of sin is immediate upon faith in Christ. And being delivered from the presence of sin is certain for the child of God too. However, being delivered from the power of sin requires our cooperation with the Spirit of God through the Word of God. If we are to be delivered more and more from the power of sin, we must have the attitude of John the Baptist: "I must decrease, and He must increase" (John 3:30). John realized this was the only way he could be useful to the Master. And so it is with us.

Are you being delivered from the power of sin? Maybe the most significant passage on how to begin to understand this is in the gospel of John.

As a young adult, I struggled with sin issues as all do. Still do, sometimes. When I was young, I didn't understand why I would have thoughts that I knew were wrong. Why was I tempted to do things I knew were sinful? Why did I do sinful things? I thought I was born again or was I?

If you don't know you can live carnally, and if you don't know God wants to deliver you from the power of sin, you will have these questions causing you to doubt. You will never be able to come up with an honest and truthful answer so that you can have the assurance of salvation.

Jesus gave His disciples a principle that we all need to understand. It was the parable of the vine:

I am the vine, and my Father is the vinedresser. Every branch in Me that does not bear fruit He takes away (Or lifts up); and

22

every branch that bears fruit He prunes, that it may bear more fruit. You are already clean because of the word I have spoken to you. Abide in Me, and I in you. As a branch cannot bear fruit of itself, unless it abides in the vine, neither can you, unless you abide in Me. I am the vine you are the branches. He who abides in Me and I in him, bears much fruit; for apart from Me you can do nothing. (John 15:1-5)

First of all, some observations about these verses:

- He was speaking to His disciples about being fruitful for the Lord, not about how to be saved from the penalty of sin.
- They were saved from the penalty of sin, "every branch in Me." A branch (disciple) can only have the potential of bearing fruit if it is part of the vine (Jesus).
- A branch bears fruit. It doesn't produce fruit.
- Apart from the vine providing all the nutrients, a branch by itself cannot bear fruit.
- Jesus is the vine. Apart from abiding in Him, disciples (branches) cannot bear fruit.

His disciples were "in Him." They were part of the vine. They were branches. But for them to bear fruit for God, they had to abide in Him. Branches can't produce any nutrients. It requires the root system of the vine to provide the things necessary to produce fruit. In the same way, Jesus will produce His fruit in us and through us if we abide in Him (the vine).

I began to realize I couldn't live the way God wanted me to because I tried to produce fruit in the old nature. That's a recipe for disaster. Focusing on yourself will cause you to lack assurance. But when I admitted that I couldn't do it, my walk started to gain some traction. He began to show me in His Word that apart from Jesus, no one can do it. The Spirit began to illuminate this truth in His Word that He lives in me and through me to produce the results. I was just a branch that could bear fruit only by abiding in Him. We bear the fruit that He produces in us when we abide in Him. When I'm not abiding, it's not possible to bear fruit for God.

Menō (Μένω) is the word in the Greek for abide. It has a wider meaning. It is translated as continue, dwell, endure, remain, stand, and tarry.[4] It paints a picture of a permanent continual close relationship with the Lord. When I stay connected to Him, I will bear fruit. However, if I depend on my own resources, I will fail to bear fruit. The power of the sin nature will control my life instead.

The vine illustration gives us a picture of abiding. In biblical, times they would place stones under the vine branches to keep them from touching the ground.[5] If the end of a branch touched the ground, it would begin to root itself. It would then draw strength from its shallow roots rather than from the primary root system. Because of the shallowness of the roots, the branches would be unable to draw the nutrients to produce acceptable fruit. Therefore, the Father as the vinedresser prunes and lifts up the vine, so it doesn't touch the ground. In doing so, the branches continue to draw from the root system and produce more fruit. He doesn't take the non-producing branches away. He lifts them up. That is the best understanding of verse two because that is His nature. He "lifts them up" as opposed to "takes away" to help them stay connected to the vine.

But the choice is yours and mine to abide: to be delivered from the power of sin. Are you willing to abide in Him? Apart from Jesus, we can bear no fruit. We will be useless and unfruitful in this life.

Unlike a vine, we have free will to make choices. Abiding is not certain for a child of God. If you as a child, live independent of Christ's influence, there is the possibility that your life will wither like a branch that fails to draw resources from the root. Withered

---

[4] Vine, Complete Expository Dictionary, 1 (New Testament).

[5] Jim Fleming, "Biblical Antiquity Center, Part 1," online video, Christ in Prophecy, https://christinprophecy.org/ sermons/biblical-antiquity-center-part-1/

branches bear no fruit for they are not drawing energy from the root (Jesus). They are useless.

There are a variety of interpretations concerning the branches being burned. Fire is not always a reference to hell. Sometimes it is used when God judges a believer's works (1 Cor. 3:15). Other times it is associated with the Holy Spirit (Acts 2:3). There's no reason to assume this is a reference to hell since it is easily established that Jesus was speaking about believers ("anyone", which includes His disciples), that are failing to abide in Him. Like withered branches that are burned, they will become useless.

Understanding the three tenses of salvation is pivotal to understanding the Bible in its proper context. It's the grace of God that provides all that we need to live godly and faithfully in this life. "His divine power has given to us all things that pertain to life and godliness" (2 Pet. 1:3). But not every believer abides in Him. None of us abide one hundred percent of the time. The power of the sin nature can control the life of a believer either by choice or by failure to understand this relational skill of abiding. Nonetheless, He preserves all believers based upon His faithfulness. And one day every believer will be delivered from the very presence of sin (1 Pet. 1:4).

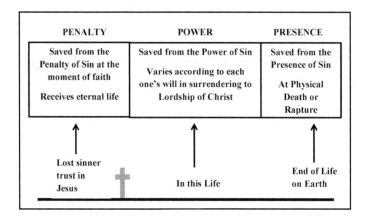

Chapter 5

A Confusing Gospel

———————➤○⌬○◅———————

The gospel is often presented as though it is a cure-all for every problem a person has. "Come to Jesus, and He will solve all your problems." So what do you do when Jesus informs us that there will be tribulations (John 16:33)? Or when James writes and says to count it all joy when various trials come your way (James 1:2)? Or when Peter encourages us not to think it strange when fiery trials happen to you (1 Pet. 4:12)? Jesus doesn't remove us from the problems, but He gives us the strength to endure if we trust Him.

"Coming to Jesus" is not an explanation of the gospel either. Jesus dealt with our sin by dying a substitutionary death. He took our place. Sin is our greatest problem and an insurmountable barrier from God. He broke down the barrier and provided the only way to be delivered from eternal condemnation, to receive forgiveness, and to be restored to fellowship with God. That's our greatest need.

It is simply not true that coming to Jesus will make all your problems go away. The apostle Paul experienced many trials and tribulations after he believed. Five times he was flogged by the Jews. Three times he was beaten with rods. He was stoned once. He was shipwrecked three times. He was in the water for a whole day and night (2 Cor. 11:24-25). God didn't remove all his problems.

If that is what you believe about the gospel, you may be looking to Jesus for the wrong reason. You may miss the truth of the gospel by seeing Jesus as a problem solver and not as your Savior from sin.

Some use the phrase, "ask Jesus in your heart", to convey the gospel. Others say "give Jesus your heart". I like to be a little facetious sometimes by asking, "Which is it? Do I ask Him in my heart or do I give Him my heart"? It's a confusing concept. What does it mean "to ask Jesus into your heart"? Once I asked a person what that meant. Upon questioning, this individual walked me through the gospel clearly. People learn that phrase when they are young. They get taught that. This person knew what it meant, but is it clear to the hearer? Communication involves both the speaker and the hearer. Does the hearer know what you mean? Most people today in America have little Biblical understanding. The average unbeliever does not know what "saved" means or even "sin." Often the simplest things have to be explained, so people understand the message of the gospel.

A few years ago, I spoke with three older teenagers at the local county fair. They lived nearby in a neighboring community. They were willing to listen to the gospel presentation. All three stayed focused on what I was saying. They were zeroed-in. When I finished, trying to gain some insight as to what they understood, I ask them if they ever heard that before. They all replied negatively. One had never been to a church. The other two had only been to church a few times in their life.

Another time I encountered a young sales lady at a local festival as she was coming around offering free beverage samples. So I engaged in conversation with her. I asked her if she was a good person and she responded that she was. I then ask her if she thought she was as good as God and she said "yes." That caught me off guard. No one ever responded to me that way before. After a brief pause, as I thought what to say, the Lord brought to mind a couple of commandments. "Have you ever lied? Have you ever

28

stolen anything?" Well, she was honest and had to admit that she had done both. "I guess I'm not as good as God," she responded. At least, I thought, now she has a little better understanding of God. That's the culture we are dealing with in America today. There is little biblical understanding of God and sin.

About thirty years ago an evangelist came to our church. He commented that sharing the gospel in America is like plowing concrete. And it is worse today than back then. Understanding the gospel is the power of the gospel. Today it usually takes a lot of time to lay the groundwork. Many people do not know the basics of Christianity anymore. Such phrases like these don't communicate truth. There's no power in the message if it's not understood.

Yes, you can ask Jesus to save you. But the Bible speaks to believing in Jesus. When you believe the gospel, understanding who He is and what He did, He gives you a new nature and indwells you with His Spirit. That's a faith response. You don't have to ask for it. It is a done deal. Jesus said, "'He who believes in Me, *as the Scripture has said*, out of his heart will flow rivers of living water.' But this He spoke concerning the Spirit, who those believing in Him would receive, for the Holy Spirit was not yet given, because Jesus was not yet glorified" (John 7:38-39, emphasis mine).

Phrases like "asking Jesus in your heart" are not found in the Bible either. Some like to use Revelation 3:20 as an invitation: "I stand at the door and knock. If anyone hears My voice and opens the door, I will come into Him and dine with him, and he with Me." If the content of the gospel is explained, people can respond to the invitation by believing the gospel. But the context of this passage is to the Laodicea church. They needed to repent. Jesus rebuked them for having a contented attitude because of their wealth. Jesus was inviting them back to fellowship. It wasn't an invitation to be saved from the penalty of sin.

As we saw in Chapter Three, sticking with biblical language is the best way to communicate the truth of God's love demonstrated in the gospel message. Jesus is the God/Man. God is holy. We are not. All of us are condemned sinners helpless to change our situation. He is our sufficient substitute. He died in our place. He rose from the grave proving He has power over sin and death. Whoever believes in Him shall not perish, but have everlasting life. You could not understand these necessary truths if I just said to you, "Ask Jesus in your heart." You could walk away believing you were on your way to heaven, when in reality you are still unsaved.

That's my concern. When someone hears a convoluted message and fails to understand the gospel, they may have the assurance of heaven when they shouldn't. We can't force people into heaven. However, our responsibility is to point them to Christ as the only way and to do so biblically and precisely. Then the responsibility is on the unbeliever to receive Him by faith or to continue in unbelief. Is Jesus merely your problem solver? Have you asked Jesus in your heart? Or have you believed the gospel, by faith alone in the person and work of the Lord Jesus Christ?

Chapter 6

The Frontloaded Gospel

Something + Jesus = Salvation???

*M*any well-meaning and maybe some not so well-meaning people communicate the gospel in a way that subtly adds work requirements to it. We cannot see a person's heart motivation, so we can only judge according to what they say. Often people do not realize what they are expressing when sharing the gospel.

Several years ago, my youngest adult son began to grow in his relationship with the Lord. He became interested in evangelism and took a popular video course at his church designed to help believers communicate the gospel. He liked it so much he even bought the video package for me that Christmas. Around the same time, my pastor had asked me to help with outreaches to our community. I sensed God working in all this, even in me to be more evangelistic. There is joy in those moments when you see an adult son or daughter becoming more and more interested in the Lord, and so I wanted to grow with him in this area of my walk.

The ministry that created the evangelism video course is popular and motivated. They do a lot of street evangelism, and I admire them for their effort in trying to reach people. They publish a wealth of tracts and tools for people around the world. I began to use their materials in my evangelism efforts and church outreaches. I even wrote some tracts that followed their methodology.

What was their methodology? Well, you would ask someone if they thought they were a good person. Most people respond by saying yes. Then you run some of the Ten Commandments by them: "Have you ever lied or stolen anything?" This should convict them that they are not good and that a good judge would come to the same conclusion. So how would they fare on Judgment Day when they stood before God? Would they go to heaven or hell? People respond to this in a number of ways. But if they say they probably would go to hell, then you have the opportunity to go through the gospel with them. That sounds like a good way, with one exception. For them to get to heaven, you must tell them that they first must repent of all their sins, meaning they must stop doing those sins, and believe the gospel.

Well, you're likely asking yourself right now, "What's wrong with that?" And at first, I thought the same thing. But something began to bother me about the tracts I was using. Did "repent of your sins" mean to acknowledge that you are a sinner? Is that what it means? Is "repenting of sins" and acknowledging myself to be a condemned sinner equal in meaning and understanding? Had I repented of all my sins (turned from all my sins)? Obviously, I had not. Since I have been a believer for over fifty-five years, most of my sins came after I got saved. Does this mean I am not saved? Are you beginning to see the problem?

This issue of repentance can get a little voluminous and complex. People have written books on the subject of repentance. But I am going to try to keep it somewhat simple and understandable. In this chapter, I am only addressing unbelievers, not believers. How does an unbeliever respond in repentance to receive Christ as Savior?

Is the Phrase "Repent of Your Sins" in the Bible?

First of all, the phrase "repent of your sins" is not in the Bible. (The New Living Translation wrongly translates "repent" to mean repent of your sins.) Another friend and I shared this with a pastor at an outreach event. He immediately pulled out his KJV Bible and began to look feverishly like a mother looking for a lost child. But after several minutes of searching and as he began to sweat profusely (it was warm in the building), he realized it was not in there. Most people, including myself in the past, think the phrase is in the Bible and most are surprised when they find out it is not. I know I was. So why do we use the phrase?

What Does the Word "Repentance" Mean?

The word "repentance" or "repent" in English does not carry with it the same meaning in Greek, the language of the New Testament. What do English-speaking people understand when you tell them to repent? I would argue most would say it means to be sorry for something that one did, to stop doing some sort of bad behavior, or a combination of both. That's not necessarily a bad thing to do, but is that what the Bible says is necessary to be saved from the penalty of sin? No. Dr. Renald Showers aptly states:

> John the Baptist (Luke 3:8) and Paul (Acts 26:20) indicate those who repent should do deeds appropriate to their repentance, but the change of conduct is the result and not the essence of repentance. In addition, Paul's statement that sorrow can prompt repentance (2 Cor. 7:9-10) implies sorrow itself is not repentance. The essence of repentance is a genuine change of mind.[6]

---

[6] Renald Showers, "The Trouble with Lordship Salvation," presented in 1990 at Word of Life Annual Conference, http://www.middletownbiblechurch.org/salvatio/lordsh10. htm

The Greek word *metanoia* (μετάνοια) means to change one's mind.[7] In conversion, it is a significant change of thinking that affects what a person believes about how to be made right with God.

A lost person must have a change of mind about what he or she believes about the person and work of Jesus Christ. Is Jesus and His work on the cross enough to save? Or must one first turn from their sins and feel sorry for them (repent)? Is Jesus necessary but not enough?

The first use of "repent" in the New Testament is in the book of Matthew. John the Baptist was preaching, "Repent for the kingdom of heaven is at hand" (Matt. 3:2). The purpose of John's ministry was to prepare the way of the Lord (Matt. 3:2). The apostle Paul makes John's message clear. He said John indeed "baptized with a baptism of repentance, saying to the people that they should *believe* on Him who would come after him; *that is on Jesus Christ*" (Acts 19:4, emphasis mine). That was John's repentance message. The Jewish people believed they were guaranteed to be in the kingdom because they were God's chosen people; because they were Jews. But John the Baptist told the Jewish leadership, "Do not think to say to yourselves, 'we have Abraham as our father.' For I say to you that God is able to raise up children to Abraham from these stones" (Matt. 3:9).

In other words, John told that generation of Jews the necessity to change their mind, their belief. He told them that they were not "okay" with God simply because they were Jewish. He was saying to them that they needed a change of mind. They needed to change their minds from believing they were children of God by ethnicity to believing in Jesus as their Messiah, their Savior from their sins.

Another time, John was baptizing when a dispute arose between his disciples and the Jews about purification (John 3:25). The Jews wanted John to agree with them and not with Jesus. But

---

[7] Vine, Complete Expository Dictionary, 525 [New Testament].

John concluded his defense of Jesus, saying, "He who believes in the Son has everlasting life; and he who does not believe the Son shall not see life, but the wrath of God abides on him" (John 3:36). Again there is no mention of repentance, only believing.

Furthermore, according to the gospel of Mark, John the Baptist preached a baptism of repentance for the remission of sins (Mark 1:4). His message as we have seen was for them to believe in Jesus as their Savior (see Acts 19:4). This was an offer to Israel through John for them to believe in Jesus as their Messiah, in order for God to restore the kingdom to them. How in the world would they receive forgiveness (remission) by repenting of their sins? No one receives judicial forgiveness for sins because they stop doing them. That would be like a judge pardoning a car thief for all his thefts because he promises he won't steal any more cars or because he is sorry for all the cars he has stolen. In either case, would a good judge be just in finding that thief not guilty? No! That wouldn't be just. Someone has to pay the penalty for the crime.

God is the ultimate perfect, righteous judge. He doesn't over-look sin because we make a pledge to stop sinning or because we feel sorry for our sin. He has made the provision at great cost to Himself. Jesus has made the ultimate payment and provision for our crimes (sins). And He instructs us to believe in Him for forgive-ness and everlasting life, because "He has appeared to put away sin by the sacrifice of Himself" (Heb. 9:26).

Repenting of Sin is Works of Righteousness

When one is told to repent of their sins, they understand they have to do something. They have to stop the bad things and do the good. This merely is works of righteousness. Doing works of righteousness is trusting in one's personal effort. It's trusting in yourself, at least in part, to save you. However, it is evident from the Bible that we are not saved, "by works of righteousness which we have done" (Titus 3:5). We are saved by Jesus Christ and His sacrifice (John 14:6)!

Frankly, when a person is told to repent of their sins, he promises God something he cannot do—turn from all his sin. So if it can't be done, then what good is it? Let's say Ralph is confronted with his sin. He especially has a problem with telling the truth. He tells a lot of lies. So now Ralph must promise God that he'll stop lying and believe in Jesus. Do you think Ralph will never tell another lie? He might have good intentions. He might be led to think he can do it. But Ralph will soon thereafter tell a lie, and if he is honest, question how he could do that as a saved person or even wonder if he really is saved, when he thought he had repented from all his sins.

Believing is the Opposite of Working

Abraham believed apart from doing any works of righteousness. In other words, he didn't repent of all his sins. He "believed God and it was accounted to him for righteousness" (Rom. 4:3). He did no works of righteousness to earn a right standing with God. He believed in the Lord and His provision. "But to him who does not work but believes on Him who justifies the ungodly, his faith is accounted for righteousness" (Rom. 4:5). The apostle Paul counted all things loss, including the righteousness from the law, that he "might gain Christ, and be found in Him, not having my own righteousness which is from the law, but that which is through faith in Christ, the righteousness which is from God by faith" (Phil. 3:7-9). He knew he needed perfect righteousness. Turning from sins (repenting) is self-righteousness when one thinks he must do this to be delivered from the penalty of sin.

Repenting of Sins vs. Admitting I am a Helpless Condemned Sinner

Repenting of sins versus acknowledging that I am a condemned sinner helpless to fix my situation are two opposite actions. Repenting is something I must do. It's works of righteousness as already explained. I am changing my behavior hoping to influence God to favor me. Admitting I am a condemned sinner helpless to fix my situation is something I believe God says about me. It is a faith response and not of works.

Believing vs. Doing

Another example of trying to do things for God was the Jews of Jesus' day. The Jewish people followed Him across the sea to Capernaum and asked Him, "What shall we do, that we may work the works of God?" Jesus answered and said to them, "This is the work of God, that you believe in Him whom He sent" (John 6:29). Man wants to do, but God says believe.

Paul and Silas were in prison in Philippi singing hymns when an earthquake opened the cell doors and freed the prisoners. The jailer was about to kill himself supposing they had fled. Paul stopped him and let him know they were still there. Then the jailer said, "Sirs, what must I do to be saved?" (Acts 16:30). There again man wants to know what he must do. The apostle did not say "clean up your act" or "quit doing this or that." He didn't even say be willing to turn from your sins. He told him to "believe on the Lord Jesus Christ, and you will be saved, you and your household" (Acts 16:31). Obviously the others in his home would have to believe, and they did. It was that simple, other than it took an earthquake to get the jailer's attention!

People repent all the time; believers and unbelievers alike. Most people feel sorry for things they do because everyone has a conscience. People change their behavior. They go to drug rehabs, or they quit smoking. This is simply reformation. It may be a good thing to do, but reformation cannot save anyone from the penalty of their sin, nor can it impart to them spiritual life. That's not biblical repentance when it comes to being delivered from the penalty of sin.

Now I realize many new believers stop sinful behaviors the moment they get saved. I have a friend who had his desire for drugs removed almost immediately. That's a good thing. But conversion doesn't happen like that for everyone. My friend still had other sins that he didn't know about at that time. And all of us, no matter how old we are, still deal with the principle of sin in our life that manifests itself in actions, whether in thoughts, words, deeds, or acts of omission. That's because we still have an old nature.

Adding Works Makes the Gospel a Different Gospel

That's how one frontloads the gospel making it another gospel, a gospel that will not save if it is believed. Doing things for Jesus will never get you into heaven, even if you are cleaning up your life.

For example, the Galatian church was influenced by the false teaching that would require them to add to the gospel. He marveled that they were "turning away so soon from Him who called you in the grace of Christ, to a different gospel" (Gal. 1:6). These false teachers perverted the gospel (Gal. 1:7). These people are called Judaizers. They tried to influence people that you had to follow the law to be saved from the penalty of sin.

Paul was so against that message that he told them, "if we or an angel from heaven, preach any other gospel to you than what we have preached to you, let him be accursed" (Gal. 1:8). In Galatians 1:8-9, the apostle declares most strongly that the gospel he preached was the one and only way of salvation, and to preach another was to nullify the death of Christ.[8]

---

[8] Vine, Complete Expository Dictionary, 141 [New Testament].

So if a person thinks they must repent of their sins, meaning to feel sorry for and to quit doing them to be saved, then he is adding to the gospel, making it a different gospel. If however, all one means by the phrase "repent of your sins" is to acknowledge one is a sinner in need of a savior, then it would be a good thing to change one's language to make it biblically clear and accurate.

The Power of the Gospel is in Understanding the Gospel

The power of the gospel is in the understanding of the gospel; "For I am not ashamed of the gospel of Christ, for it is the *power* of God to salvation for everyone who believes, for the Jew first and also for the Greek [Gentile]" (Rom. 1:16, emphasis mine). The word here for "power" is *dunamis* [δύναμις] in the Greek. It's the same word translated as "'meaning" in 1 Corinthians 14:11: "Therefore if I do not know the *meaning* of the language, I will be a foreigner to him who speaks, and he who speaks will be a foreigner to me" (emphasis mine). It is interesting that the same word translated "power" is also translated as "meaning" in reference to language. There is power in understanding the meaning of the language.

Since the gospel is communicated with language, it is essential that we communicate accurately. For example, in today's world, many new things have to be assembled. Usually, there are directions that are often written in several different languages. How could you follow any directions if all you had were German instructions, not knowing that language? There would be no power in those directions for you. However, directions in your language give you all the power you need to follow the instructions.

Similarly, the wrong language causes a confusing gospel presentation and lacks power in its saving message, because it may not be adequately understood. It also emphasizes the wrong object to save. Frontloading the gospel places emphasis on you cleaning up your act rather than on the person and work of Christ.

Repentance is Not Found in the Gospel of John

It's also curious that repentance is not found in the entire gospel of John. This is significant because one of the purposes of the gospel of John was evangelistic, to lead people to salvation through Christ. "But these things are written that you may believe that Jesus is the Christ, the Son of God, and that believing you may have life in His name" (John 20:31). John used the word "believe" many times throughout his gospel, but he never used the word "repent" even one time (John 3:15-16; 18; 36; 4:48, 53; 5:24; 6:29, 35, 40, 47; etc.). It is odd that if repenting of sins was even part of the issue in salvation (deliverance from the penalty of sin), that he would have used it along with believing and faith. This is probably due to the fact that he saw a person who had believed in Jesus as one who had repented—one who had a change of mind about the person and work of the Lord Jesus.

Other Terminology for "Repenting of Your Sins"

Repenting of sins is often couched in other terminology as well. Some will say "you need to turn from all your sin or to be willing to turn from your sins, or you need to feel sorry for your sins." What if you didn't feel sorry? What if you still sin? Have you turned from all of them? And if you haven't turned from all your sin, did you honestly repent of them? Telling an unbeliever that he must "repent of his sins" is simply making an agreement with God that he or she cannot keep. A sinner is promising God to stop sinning to receive God's promise of forgiveness and eternal life. If the sinner is honest, he realizes not long after that his promise to stop sinning is a promise that he cannot keep. In essence, they are telling people to stop sinning, which is impossible. Have you stopped sinning? It's a dilemma that no one can live up to.

All are Helpless and Condemned Sinners

Indeed, an unbeliever must understand that he is a sinner. Almost everyone I have ever talked to knows this. They don't necessarily use the word "sin" or "sinner." But they do say things like, "No one is perfect" or "Everyone makes mistakes." What the unbeliever needs to understand is that they are not just a sinner, but they are a condemned sinner and helpless to fix their situation.

No one can receive forgiveness or restore their fellowship with God by self-effort. That's what most people do not realize and fail to believe about themselves. Most believe God will accept them because they tried to do their best. But that won't get you anywhere with Him on Judgment Day, because in comparison to Him, there is none good, not even one (Rom. 3:12).

Summary

Repentance means "a change of mind." If the context is used about eternal life, sin is not the issue. A change in belief is. When sin is the object of repentance, eternal life is not the issue. Believers need to repent to maintain fellowship with God, to glorify God, and to avoid the consequences of sin.

Everyone at some point is bent on doing good works to get to heaven. That's our brokenness and makeup as humans. Evangelists feed that need of the unbeliever when they tell them that they need to turn (repent) from their sins to get saved. In doing so, they are adding requirements to the gospel, thereby making it another gospel. Can't we trust the Spirit of God to begin to work in the person to show him the areas of life that need to be changed after one is saved?

When one tells an unbeliever to repent of their sins, they are telling them to stop the bad things they are doing and to do good. It's the thing they usually have tried to convince them that they are not—good! It's telling them they have to be good so they can receive forgiveness from the Lord. Frontloading the gospel is putting the cart before the horse. It's telling an unbeliever they need to be sanctified to be justified.

Maybe you lack assurance because you have heard such a message. This frontloaded message focuses you on yourself and not on Christ. Fix your attention instead on the Lord Jesus Christ. He paid for all of your sins on the cross and has imputed His perfect righteousness to you the moment you trusted in Him alone (2 Cor. 5:21). Take God at His word. Only then will you have assurance.

Wrong Gospel vs. Right Gospel		
#1 Wrong Gospel:	**Something + Faith in Jesus = salvation**	
(Front Loading)	Repenting of sins	
	Change Behavior	
	Promise to be good	
	Self- effort	
#2 Right Gospel:	**Nothing + Faith in Jesus = salvation**	

Chapter 7

The Backloaded Gospel

Jesus + Something = Salvation???

Many of those who frontload the gospel also backload the gospel. In other words, they will evaluate the Christian walk after one is saved as a plumb line as to whether one is saved or not. If you are not living in a godly way according to their judgment, then they assign you as a "professing" believer or a "false" believer. According to back-loaders, you must show evidence of your salvation by good works and godly living. Their mantra is "you'll know them by their fruits," a quotation from Matthew 7. But Matthew is speaking about false prophets, and it is the fruit of the lips, what they say, that identifies them as false prophets. Their behavior may disqualify them as a prophet (teacher) and leader, but it's not their behavior that makes one a false prophet. It's what they teach.

The problem with backloading theology is that it blends justification and sanctification truths. Justification occurs at the moment when a sinner believes the gospel. At that time, God declares the believing sinner righteous, not guilty. The perfect righteousness of Christ is credited to him. "But now the righteousness of God apart from the law is revealed… even the righteousness of God through faith in Jesus Christ, to all and on all who believe" (Rom. 3:21-22). If you have believed the gospel, then you have a right standing before God. You are justified. It's a one and done deal.

Sanctification, however, is a life-long pursuit. Although you have a position of being sanctified at the moment of faith, it is also to be lived out in this life by God's grace through faith as well. The first one is referred to as positional sanctification. God sees the sinner who has believed as holy (1 Cor. 1:2, 6:11).

But in life, the believer continues to sin. So much of the New Testament is written to believers to exhort them to live a sanctified life, a life that is set apart to God. "For this is the will of God, your sanctification" (1 Thess. 4:3). And Peter exhorted, "but as He who called you is holy, you also be holy in all your conduct" (1 Pet. 1:15). Practical sanctification is life long, and no one ever arrives entirely on this side of eternity.

A typical back-loader of the gospel implies that justification guarantees sanctification. In other words, if you are saved, you will show it by your good works and righteous living. Not only that, but you will persevere in faith to the end of your life. But all this does is place the burden on you rather than learning to rest in and trust the Lord in the moments of time and the circumstances of life, "looking unto Jesus the author and finisher of our faith" (Heb. 12:2).

Rather than living a life out of gratitude because of God's love, mercy, and grace, it causes one to live a life of fear of not pleasing the Lord or even fear of not being accepted by Him. As a younger man who lacked much wisdom and understanding, I also wondered if you could lose your salvation. And had I lost mine? There indeed are passages that indicate that, like Hebrews 6 and 10. But a close examination of those passages will show that they are written to believers who are eternally secure.

The biblical truth is once you are known by God in a relational way by believing in the gospel, you cannot lose your relationship. But backloading the gospel like this can make you question yourself and cause you to have little or no assurance, the very thing the Lord wants us to know. He doesn't want to keep us in the dark until Judgment Day. He has plainly told us that if we trust in His Son, we have everlasting life. "These things I have written to you who believe in the name of the Son of God so *that you may know you have eternal life*" (1 John 5:13, emphasis mine). If there were something that you could do to forfeit eternal life, then it wouldn't be eternal, would it? It would only be temporary life.

Backloading, like frontloading, subtly places the burden on you to be good enough to ensure you are truly saved. They have the right language, and it sounds good—you're saved by grace through faith apart from works, but if you're not working or performing they may write you out of heaven as a false believer. But it's comforting to know that God doesn't.

Does God want us to do good works and to live righteously? Absolutely! "Shall we continue in sin that grace may abound? Certainly not!" (Rom. 6:1-2). But He doesn't require us to do these things to stay saved or to help save us from the penalty of sin. They should flow as a result of gratitude as one grows in the understanding of His love, mercy, and grace. Grace is a much better motivator than Law.

As a believer, God doesn't demand you live righteously, but He desires you to do so out of love for Him, out of gratitude of what He has done for you. It's His grace that teaches us that "we should live soberly, righteously, and godly in the present age" (Titus 2:12). And learning to do this takes time, understanding, effort, and desire because right out of the gate, we are bent on living a self-dependent life rather than a God-dependent life.

Good works and righteous living is not a barometer of whether a person is saved or not. Many people live outwardly righteous and good lives that do not believe in the Lord as Savior. Actually, if one thinks entrance is gained by doing good works, then it is likely that they will work diligently to gain entrance to heaven.

Jesus spoke of many who will call Him Lord proclaiming their works that they did: prophesied, cast out demons, and did many wonders in His name. But He will respond to them, "I never knew you, depart from Me, you who practice lawlessness" (Matt. 7:21-23). They had done great and wonderful things in the name of Jesus, but they were denied entrance into the kingdom of heaven. Why? They had trusted in their self-righteousness, their works rather than in the Him and His work on their behalf.

Backloading the gospel changes the gospel message from being "good news" to not so good news, because you can't know for sure if you will make it to heaven. No one can define what it means to persevere in faith and good works till the day you die. For example, consider the following illustrations of a fictional guy named Bill. Let's say he's struggling with life. Nothing is going right for him. Because of his bad marriage and problems with his children, he begins to drink. At the same time, one of his coworkers has been witnessing to him about the Lord, that we're all sinners in need of a savior. So one day Bill is on his way to work, listening to a pastor on the radio sharing the salvation of God through faith in His Son Jesus Christ. He understands his need. And at that moment, he believes in Christ to save him from his sin and to give him everlasting life.

In the emotion and intensity of the moment, Bill is distracted and passes through a stop sign at a busy intersection. When he passes through the intersection, he is broadsided and killed. Did Bill go to heaven?

A second scenario is that Bill gets saved that morning and begins to attend church once in a while. He starts to read the Bible but doesn't grow much because he continues to struggle with family life problems. Six months later, traveling down the road, he's distracted by his problems, and as he passes through that intersection without stopping, he's broadsided and killed. Did Bill go to heaven?

A third scenario is that Bill gets saved on the way to work one morning while listening to a clear gospel presentation on the radio. He begins to attend church sporadically and tries to read his Bible. However, he is never able to give up his drinking habit, and his marriage ends in divorce. Distracted by all this, he quits going to church and stops reading his Bible. Six years down the road he is diagnosed with a terminal disease, likely because of his drinking over the years. Driving to work he is distracted in his mind over all his problems, passes through the intersection without stopping, and is killed. Did Bill go to heaven?

How you answer these three questions should give you an idea of how well you understand God's grace. Bill believed the gospel and his assurance should have been in the death, burial, and resurrection of the Lord Jesus. Jesus paid for all of Bill's sins on the cross. At the moment he believed, he received the forgiveness of sins, was restored to a relationship with God, was made fit for heaven with the perfect righteousness of Christ, and received everlasting life as a free gift. Bill's good performance or bad performance, after he was saved, could never affect his eternal destination in heaven whether he died that day, six months later, or six years later. But what Bill's life actions did affect was his fellowship with the Lord.

Frontloading or backloading the gospel message confuses and changes the gospel message. It emphasizes the sinner not to believe the gospel, but to change his or her behavior to get saved or to give assurance to one's self that I am saved. If you heard the gospel from a front-loader or back-loader, you could never be one hundred percent sure you are going to heaven. Did you repent of all your sins? Have you turned from all your sins? Will you remain faithful all of your life? What if you died in a period of unfaithfulness or disobedience?

The only gospel is the person and work of the Lord Jesus Christ. He did everything necessary to reconcile sinners to Himself. When one understands one's helpless situation as a condemned sinner, then the only thing one needs to do is to believe, to rely on Him alone for salvation. When one does, God says that person has ever-lasting life (John 3:16, 6:47). Believe His word, and you will have assurance. Trust in yourself, and you won't.

Baptism

Others backload the gospel by adding religious rituals like baptism and communion, teaching that such things are necessary for salvation too. But those are works added on by man. Jesus commanded believers to be baptized and to partake in communion. Baptism identifies the believer with the death, burial, and resurrection of our Lord (Rom. 6:3-5). In communion we are reminded of what Christ has done for us. We are proclaiming His death until He comes (1 Cor. 11:24-26). But such things don't help get you in to heaven.

Once I shared the gospel with a young woman at a fair ministry booth. After I finished, I asked her if she were sure she would go to heaven. She confidently said yes. That was pleasing to hear that a Christian was one hundred percent sure of heaven, I thought. Then just to be certain she understood the gospel, I asked her what she would say to God in order to let her in. (I'm sure entrance to heaven doesn't happen this way, but it helps to find out what a person is trusting in.) Without hesitation, she said she was baptized!

When I delved a little deeper into her understanding, I found she went to a church in a denomination that teaches that you must be baptized to go to heaven. She had entirely missed the gospel message.

Believers' baptism should be an act of obedience once a person is saved from the penalty of sin, but it's not a requirement to get to heaven. The apostle Paul, the greatest evangelist, thanked God that he didn't baptize many of those in Corinth except for a few (1 Cor. 1:14-16). That would be odd if he wanted to see them saved. He obviously knew it wasn't a matter of eternal consequence. In fact, he said Christ did not send him to baptize, but to preach the gospel (1 Cor. 1:17). Then in the next verse, he states, "the message of the cross is foolishness to those who are perishing, but to us who are being saved it is the power of God" (v. 18). People get saved by hearing the message of the cross and believing in the person and work of Christ, not by being baptized.

The thief on the cross was not baptized, but when he asked Jesus to remember him when He came into His kingdom, Jesus told him, "Today you will be with Me in Paradise" (Luke 23:42-43). "Therefore we conclude that a man is justified by faith apart from the deeds of the law" (Rom. 3:28). We become children of God by faith in Jesus Christ alone (Gal. 3:26; John 1:12), not by baptism. Remission of sins only come through Jesus Christ (Acts 10:43).

Adding baptism or any other thing to the gospel makes it a different gospel. My prayer is that the lady I spoke to went away with the right understanding. Misunderstanding what saves is a matter of eternal consequences.

In summary, have you believed the backloaded gospel? Maybe you have assurance in the wrong thing. The gospel is simple; Jesus said, "Most assuredly, I say to you, he who believes in Me has everlasting life" (John 6:47). There is only one way. Jesus said, "I am the way, the truth, and the life. No one comes to the Father except through Me" (John 14:6). And Jesus did all that is necessary: "Christ died for our sins according to the Scriptures, and that He was buried, and that He rose again the third day according to the Scriptures" (1 Cor. 15:3-4). Only then is the gospel powerful and effective to save. The apostle Paul wrote, "For I am not ashamed of the gospel of Christ, for it is the power of God to salvation for everyone who believes, for the Jew first and also for the Greek" (Rom. 1:16). It is only in His shed blood that we have redemption, the forgiveness of sins, according to the riches of His grace (Eph. 1:7).

Causing one to look at his or her performance to determine salvation will only lead to a misplaced assurance or create doubt. If you are a believer, focusing on yourself and your behavior will frustrate you till the day you die. It's the very thing that the devil wants you to do. Because when you take your eyes off Christ and put them on yourself, you have no power to live a fruitful and functional life for the Lord. And when someone adds to the message of the gospel, it changes the message to a different gospel, a gospel that will not save a person, if it is believed.

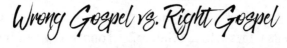

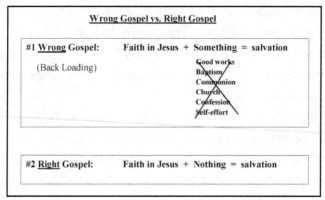

Chapter 8

Two or Three Chairs Theology

———⋙o⟨⟨⟨⟩⟩o⟨———

M ost back-loaders and front-loaders have only "two chairs" theology. I know you're asking, "What in the world are you talking about?" Well, let me try to paint you a picture in your mind. Envision three chairs facing the congregation from the front of the church. The chair on the right represents an unbeliever. The chair in the middle represents a believer out of fellowship with God, living independently of God's control. The Bible calls such a person carnal (I Corinthians 3:1, 3). The chair on the left represents a believer walking in the Spirit, in close communion with God. Is that not what you see in Scripture—believers living spiritually, believers living badly, and unbelievers?

But the front and back-loaders don't have a middle chair in their theology. They only have two chairs: saved and unsaved. There is no room in their belief system for someone who may fall away from the church or even from the faith or sin too much. They do allow you to experience some sin, but you will always return to faith and obedience. I believe most of the people who teach this are well-meaning and want what's best for their congregation or group. But having good intentions doesn't make it right.

They base their theology on the faulty assumption that all "true" believers will persevere to the end of life in faith and obedience. For example, one popular study Bible comments on 2 Timothy

2:12, "Believers who persevere give evidence of the genuineness of their faith."[9] But that's only something that God can know because only He can see the belief and motivation of the heart of a person. "For man looks at the outward appearance, but the Lord looks at the heart" (1 Sam. 16:7).

Furthermore, why does the Bible exhort believers to persevere if it were automatic? Peter exhorts believers to add to their faith perseverance to be useful and fruitful (2 Pet. 1:6, 8). The writer to the Hebrews tells them that they have need of endurance so they can do the will of God (Heb. 10:36). The reason Christians are instructed to persevere and endure is that the natural inclination is to give up, especially when things get tough. Perseverance is developed by positively responding to the trials in life by faith in the Lord and His word (Rom. 5:3, 10:17).

A second reason these people have only a two-chairs theology is that they deny the power of the old nature in the believer or they deny that the believer still has an old nature. This same study Bible comments, "The believer does not have two competing natures, the old and the new, but one new nature that is still incarcerated in unredeemed flesh."[10] I'm not even sure what that means, other than it is a denial that the power of the old nature can still control a believer.

But the Bible affirms that the old nature still resides in every child of God. It doesn't cease to exist nor does it improve. It is still deceitful above all things and desperately wicked (Jer. 17:9). When a person is born again, God gives him a new nature, but He doesn't remove the old nature. That's why the apostle Paul wrote to the church at Ephesus to put off the old man and to put on the new man which was created according to God in true righteousness and holiness (Eph. 4:22-24). That's why he told the brethren in the Galatian church that "the flesh lusts against the Spirit and the

---

[9] John MacArthur, The MacArthur Study Bible (Nashville London Vancouver Melbourne: Word Bibles 1997), 1877 [Note on 2 Timothy 2:12].

[10] MacArthur, The MacArthur Study Bible, 1703 [Note on Romans 6:6].

Spirit against the flesh, and these are contrary to one another, so that you do not do the things that you wish" (Gal. 5:17). If a believer could no longer be controlled by the old nature, there would be no struggle with sin. And if all you had were the new nature which is created in true righteousness and holiness, then it would be impossible to sin. You could not and would not sin. The new nature is incapable of sinning.

Yet believers do sin and do so sometimes worse than unbelievers because both have a sin nature and are capable of doing the same things. Even an unbeliever, having only the sin nature, can go to church for years. They can help out at the local soup kitchen and may give financially to good causes. They can even read the Bible and go on mission trips. And vice versa, believers can do the things that unbelievers do. Believers are still capable of committing the same kind of sin they did as an unbeliever.

For example, King David had Uriah sent to the frontline in battle so that he would be killed to hide the fact that he had an adulterous relationship with Uriah's wife because she had become pregnant with the king's baby. And he didn't readily admit to his sin (2 Sam. 11-12). Many commentators believe it was a year minimally until Nathan the prophet confronted him before he confessed his sin. So for at least a year, David, a man after God's own heart, had lived in sin out of fellowship with the Lord. How is that possible, if there is no middle chair in which to sit?

After David, his son Solomon became king and he built the temple of the Lord. The Lord spoke to him in a dream (1 Kings 3:5-14). The Lord gave him his request of a wise and understanding heart and also gave him what he had not asked for, riches and honor. At the dedication of the temple, Solomon prayed, "Lord God of Israel, there is no God in heaven above or on earth below like you" (1 Kings 8:23); and "that all the peoples of the earth may know that the Lord is God; there is no other" (v. 60). Solomon also authored the books of Ecclesiastes, Song of Solomon, and many biblical proverbs. There should be no question that Solomon had a relationship with the Lord.

So then when he became old, how could his wives turn his heart after other gods so that his heart was not loyal to the Lord his God if there is no middle chair (1 Kings 11:3-4)? He certainly didn't persevere to the end of his life in faith and obedience. So according to "two chairs" theology, he must have been a "professing" believer, not a "true" believer. But that doesn't fit the biblical narrative. He sat down in the middle chair of carnality at the end of his life. He was led astray by his wives when he was old. One of Solomon's own proverbs says, "The righteous should choose his friends carefully, for the way of the wicked leads them astray" (Prov. 12:26). As a child of God, he significantly failed because he dismissed God's instructions for him and was led away by the wicked.

Another example is Samson. He was a judge of Israel and is listed in the faith chapter of Hebrews 11. He was blessed of the Lord (Judg. 13:24). But he certainly failed to live godly throughout much of his life. He lived much of the time carnally, letting his lusts and anger control him. He is known for seeking out relationships with women of questionable character (Judg. 16:1). His relationship with Delilah, a woman from Philistia, the enemy of Israel, led to his demise. What many Philistine men could not do, a single woman was able to do. Was Samson a saved man destined for heaven? Or was he a false believer? Or was he a man who started with a relationship with the Lord, but struggled much of the time to live a life that glorified God, because he chose to sit down in that middle chair? I would argue that he was a man that sat in the middle chair much of his life. He chose to live carnally as a believer.

A fourth example is a man in the Corinthian church that had a sexual relationship with his father's wife! Paul stated such a sin was not even named among the Gentiles (1 Cor. 5:1). The church had not dealt with it, and the apostle made it clear that it was a serious thing to overlook. He advised them that the church doesn't judge those outside the church, but it was their duty to judge such sin committed by someone that was part of the church (1 Cor. 5:12). They were to administer biblical discipline. Biblical discipline is for the purpose of correcting and restoring a brother or sister back to fellowship with God and with one another (Gal. 6:1). The church is not to discipline the unbeliever in the world. The church is to evangelize them. The point is that the apostle didn't conclude the sinning brother was unsaved, but that he acted carnally and needed to be dealt with firmly as a believer. If there is no middle chair to sit in, then what do you conclude about him? He must be lost—an unbeliever.

And last of all, if the church doesn't discipline its members, then God just might. He judged many in the Corinthian church. "For this reason, many of you are weak and sick among you, and many sleep" (1 Cor. 11:30). Many died before their time—believers who went home early because of their carnality!

The middle chair is the position of carnality. What is carnality? Carnality is the state of a believer who is still immature in the faith when one should have grown up. For example, the Corinthians were saved and by that time should have grown up to spiritual maturity. However, the apostle Paul identified them not as spiritual but as babes in Christ (1 Cor. 3:1). He said they were carnal (1 Cor. 3:3). They did not choose to live out of the new nature. As a baby is unable to eat meat, so the Corinthian church was unable to digest solid spiritual food. They still needed to eat like a baby Christian, not because they were new in the faith, but because they failed to grow to any degree of spiritual maturity.

As a result, there were arguments among them concerning silly things such as who baptized them (1:11). It also created envy, strife, and division among them (3:3). A man slept with his father's wife (5:1). They brought lawsuits against one another (6:1). They were told to flee immorality and idolatry (6:18, 10:14). Some were drunk when they participated in the Lord's Supper (11:21). They were ignorant of spiritual things (12:1). In fact, in his second letter to the Corinthian church, the apostle Paul mourned for those who failed to be sanctified, "for many who have sinned before and have not repented of the uncleanness, fornication, and lewdness which they have practiced" (2 Cor. 12:21).

Every Christian will respond carnally at times to various trials and temptations. But carnality will not rule the mature Christian's life. The mature Christian has learned to develop his relationship with the Lord so that his or her responses are more and more controlled through the influence of the Spirit of God through the word of God by faith. The mature believer has learned not to let sin reign in his body, to obey it in its lust (Rom. 6:12). But that takes time, and it is a day by day and moment by moment decision. Plus, it is easy to fall back into carnality, if one is not diligent in pursuing his or her relationship with the Lord by faith.

In summary, there are many today that deny, ignore, or downplay the significance and power of the old nature and carnality in the believer. They have "two chairs" theology. This will ultimately lead to confusion in the pews. It may cause you to doubt your salvation, keeping you from living a fruitful and abundant life. And it fails to teach those in carnality a way out. It can also lead believers acting carnally to be judgmental, legalistic, and think that their actions are right when in reality they are not. To deny that Christians cannot live carnally is to deny a large portion of Scripture.

Because one can only act carnally when living out of the old nature, much of the New Testament is directed toward believers instructing them not to live like the world. Believers are to walk in the Spirit and to grow in the grace and knowledge of our Lord and Savior Jesus Christ (1 John 2:15; Gal. 5:16; 2 Pet. 3:18). This can only happen when the believer surrenders his will to God's through the power of the Holy Spirit by faith. This is the solution for the believer that lives carnally in the middle chair, not to deny the existence or the power of the old nature.

Believers' Two Natures

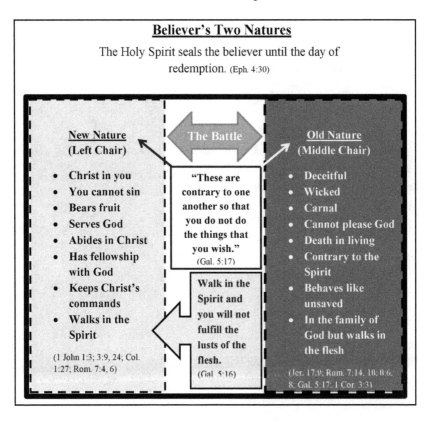

Believer's Two Natures

The Holy Spirit seals the believer until the day of redemption. (Eph. 4:30)

New Nature
(Left Chair)

The Battle

Old Nature
(Middle Chair)

- Christ in you
- You cannot sin
- Bears fruit
- Serves God
- Abides in Christ
- Has fellowship with God
- Keeps Christ's commands
- Walks in the Spirit

(1 John 1:3; 3:9, 24; Col. 1:27; Rom. 7:4, 6)

"These are contrary to one another so that you do not do the things that you wish." (Gal. 5:17)

Walk in the Spirit and you will not fulfill the lusts of the flesh. (Gal. 5:16)

- Deceitful
- Wicked
- Carnal
- Cannot please God
- Death in living
- Contrary to the Spirit
- Behaves like unsaved
- In the family of God but walks in the flesh

(Jer. 17:9; Rom. 7:14, 18; 8:6, 8; Gal. 5:17; 1 Cor. 3:3)

57

Chapter 9

Fellowship with God

—————————◦⟨⟨⟨⟨∕⟩⟩⟩◦⟨———————————

I f you are walking in the Spirit, you are in fellowship with God. The Bible uses the same words that describe human relationships as it does to describe believers in relationship with God. The believer is called a child of God (John 1:12) and also referred to as little children (1 John 2:1). The Lord said we would be called His sons and daughters (2 Cor. 6:18). God is often referred to as our Father (Gal. 1:4, 4:6). This terminology alone implies a believer is in a relationship with the Lord and can have fellowship with Him.

There is a distinction between relationship and fellowship. Relationship speaks to my position as a child of God in justification and indwelt by the Holy Spirit. Fellowship speaks to my condition as a child of God in sanctification when I am being led by the Spirit.[11]

Furthermore, the Bible says we can know God relationally. Jesus prayed, "*this is eternal life that they may know You*, the only true God, and Jesus Christ whom you have sent" (John 17:3, emphasis mine).

Eternal life is not only a never-ending life, but it is also a quality of life that is defined by knowing God. It's life that can begin to be experienced now in fellowship with God through the word

---

[11] David R. Anderson, Bewitched – The Rise of Neo-Galatianism, (USA: Grace Theology Press, 2015), 105.

of God by faith. When I read and study the Word, I develop my understanding of God's character and how He has interacted with people over the years. The Scriptures teach me that He is kind to the unthankful and evil (Luke 6:35). He is gracious and full of compassion, slow to anger, and great in mercy (Ps. 145:8). He is love (1 John 4:8). He is holy (Isa. 6:3). Great is His faithfulness (Lam. 3:23). His greatness is unsearchable (Ps. 145:3) He exercises lovingkindness, judgment, and righteousness in the earth (Jer. 9:24). And you could go on and on about the attributes and character of God. He's infinite! His Word teaches me to depend on Him: "Casting all your cares upon Him, for He cares for you" (1 Pet. 5:7).

We can develop a close personal relationship with Him just as we can develop close personal relationships with people. But it takes time and effort getting to know Him through His Word and acting upon it by faith. I enter a relationship with Him the moment I trust in Jesus as my personal Savior. Then I should learn to grow, to know Him to greater and greater depths. This is fellowship or close personal intimacy. It's learning to walk by faith, not by sight, trusting Him to direct and guide your path (Ps. 119:105). Paul's prayer for the church at Ephesus was that they would be "strengthened with might through His Spirit in the inner man; that Christ may dwell in your hearts through faith" and that they "may be able to comprehend with all the saints what is the width and length and depth and height—to know the love of God which passes knowledge; that you may be filled with all the fullness of God" (Eph. 3:16-19). Because the Spirit of God lives in each and every believer, we can grow to know God to greater and greater depths. Paul's prayer was that they would know the Lord in a deep and personal way.

But why don't we? What prevents our fellowship with God? It's that little three letter word: sin. More particularly, it is unconfessed sin and failure to walk in the light. Sin is anything we do in thought, word, or deed that God says is wrong. But it can also be things that we don't do that we should do—sins of omission. Not all sin is blatant like that of David and his sin with Bathsheba either. Many times it is more deceptive by participating in culturally acceptable practices. For example, there are a lot of Christians that live together before marriage and engage in its intimacy, believing it is an acceptable lifestyle before God. But it isn't. God calls it fornication. It's a serious sin. Paul wrote to the church at Ephesus to "let it not be named among you, as is fitting for the saints" (Eph. 5:3). A child of God cannot have fellowship with God while living such a lifestyle. "If we say that we have fellowship with Him and walk in darkness, we lie and do not practice the truth" (1 John 1:6).

However, the believer can be restored to fellowship by confessing his sin and forsaking it. "If we confess our sins, he is faithful and just to forgive us our sins and to cleanse us from all unrighteousness" (1 John 1:9). The context of the book of 1 John is fellowship of the believer with the Lord. It speaks of relational forgiveness. It's similar to when you as a child had done something wrong. You lost fellowship temporarily with your mother or father until correction was made and you acknowledged you were wrong. Like God, a good parent might administer discipline (Heb. 12:5), but ultimately fellowship was restored. You never lost the relationship though. You didn't cease to be your parent's child, but there became a breach in fellowship until confession and correction were made. And likewise, a child of God can never lose his or her relationship. However, a believer can lose their fellowship.

Unbelievers are not in a relationship with the Lord. They can't have fellowship. Fellowship can only be experienced by one who has come to know God by faith in Jesus Christ. First John is speaking to believers to acknowledge their sin and to walk in the light in order to be restored to fellowship (1 John 1:6-7). Still, you have some out there who teach that a child of God can't walk in darkness. For example, one Bible commentary states, "A genuine believer walks habitually in the light [truth and holiness], not in darkness [falsehood and sin]."[12] I would agree that believers should walk this way, but not all believers do. No one does one hundred percent of the time. Why would the apostle Paul write to the believers at Ephesus: *"have no fellowship with the unfruitful works of darkness*, but rather expose them" (Eph. 5:11, emphasis mine)? If a "genuine" believer walks habitually in the light, then why would Paul have to warn them not to have any fellowship with works of darkness?

Why would he write to the believers in the church at Rome to, *"cast off the work of darkness*, and let us put on the armor of light. Let us walk properly, as in the day, not in revelry and drunkenness, not in lewdness and lust, not in strife and envy" (Rom. 13:12-13, emphasis mine)? "Walking" here describes a way of life, not just occasional sins. Why would they be told not to live in these sinful ways, if it were not possible for them to do so?

Teaching people that a "genuine" believer walks habitually in holiness and not in darkness almost guarantees they will fall short. It teaches believers to live a "have to life" rather than a "thank you" life.[13] Believers will be motivated to live to please God by good behavior driven by the flesh rather than by the Spirit. Or one will be unprepared for the spiritual warfare that will come your way. It sets up the believer for failure in living this life by faith.

"Habitual" is a subjective term as well. What constitutes a habit? How many times do you have to sin before you are a habitual sinner? Is sinning once a day in thought, word, or deed habitual? If it is, we're all in big trouble. What if you are an introspective person? Trying to determine if you have sinned habitually could drive such a one to the brink of insanity. Again these are teachings that compel you to look at yourself rather than looking to the Savior by faith.

---

[12] MacArthur, The MacArthur Study Bible, 1964.

[13] Anderson, Bewitched, 203.

Even the church at Corinth was called into fellowship with the Lord despite all of their carnality (1 Cor. 1:9). They certainly had some ongoing issues with "habitual" sin. But their relationship didn't depend on their walk. Their fellowship did. They were saved, and they came into fellowship with God. They fell into some major sin issues, and they lost fellowship. There are consequences for living out of fellowship. Many of them were weak, many were sick, and many of them died early because God judged them (1 Cor. 11:30). But their eternal destination was not affected. God's grace extends not only to the worst unbeliever, but it also extends to the worst sinning believer as well. How could it not?

I am not endorsing sinful living. We should put on "the Lord Jesus Christ, and make no provision for the flesh, to fulfill its lust" (Rom. 13:14). But some folks paint an unrealistic picture of life as a Christian. "Genuine" believers do not always walk in holiness. We should, but we do not. When a believer walks in darkness, he or she does so because they choose to walk in the flesh and not in the Spirit. When you walk in the flesh you are not in fellowship with the Lord. We make choices in life. And our choices have consequences. This could be the reason you lack assurance because you are walking in darkness.

Realize that fellowship is described a number of ways in Scripture. It is walking in the Spirit, entering His rest, abiding in Christ, walking in the light, and keeping His commands (Gal. 5:16; Heb. 4:10; 1 John 2:5-6; Eph. 5:8). When you are living out of the resources of the new nature, you cannot sin. This isn't, nor can it be, done by self-effort. That's why God has graciously given the believer a new nature in-dwelt by the Spirit of God.

No one can live the Christian life apart from depending on the Spirit of God through the Word of God. The Spirit gives the believer the power and even the desire to do the things of God. But it requires surrendering to God by faith in those moments of time by depending on His help and strength. "For we do not have a High

Priest who cannot sympathize with our weaknesses, but was in all points tempted as we are, yet without sin. Let us therefore come boldly to the throne of grace, that we may obtain mercy and find grace to help in the time of need" (Heb. 4:15-16).

Going back to the chair illustration, when you are in fellowship you are sitting in the third chair. However, when you are not in fellowship, you have sat down on that middle chair living life independent of God's influence. As a child of God, you haven't lost your salvation, but you have lost your fellowship. Your loss of fellowship may affect your sense of assurance, but not your final destination in heaven.

Believer's Relationship vs. Fellowship

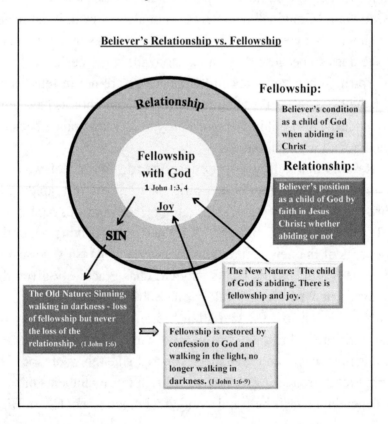

Chapter 10

Everlasting Life: Reward or Gift

———————◦⟨⟩◦———————

*A*good friend and I have debated this issue of rewards for a while. He doesn't easily give in to an opposing argument, and I am good with that. One day another friend called him a curmudgeon, and he liked it, and so it stuck. But the dictionary definition of curmudgeon doesn't describe him. According to *Webster's World Dictionary*, a curmudgeon is a surly, ill-mannered, bad-tempered person; cantankerous man. He doesn't fit that description. He's more of a strong-willed, non-conforming, truthful, sometimes impatient, straight-to-the-point kind of guy. If you want to know what he thinks, just ask him, and he'll give you an answer.

Anyway, when our discussion on rewards began, he had concluded every believer in Christ will hear, "Well done, good and faithful servant. Enter into the joy of your Lord." I listened and asked questions. I wasn't sure that I agreed, but at the time, I could not prove it from Scripture. And my opinion was not a satisfactory argument with him. He always says opinions are like rear ends. Everyone has one. If you don't show him the Scripture, he's not going to listen to you. I thank God for his friendship and influence in my life. Everyone needs an iron sharpener.

So over the years I studied, discussed, and debated. My conclusion is that reward is for faithful believers because the "well done" is given to those who have been true to the Lord's instructions:

"You were faithful over a few things; I will make you ruler over many things" (Matt. 25:21, 23). Not all servants (believers) are faithful in life, but all believers enter into the joy of the Lord.

In my uninformed years when my spiritual growth was stagnant, I believed, like many, that the reward is getting to go to heaven. But getting to go to heaven—in other words, everlasting life—is a gift (Rom. 6:23). It's not a reward. They are two distinct biblical truths. And it makes a big difference when they are not correctly understood.

For example, you could use a verse like Hebrews 10:35, "Therefore do not cast away your confidence which has great reward," to mean you could lose your salvation or you must persevere in faith and obedience to the end of life to stay saved. But "reward" here is speaking to believers to remain faithful, so that they would receive a great reward at the judgment seat of Christ.

There's much out there written about what these rewards are, and I'm not going to try to tackle that issue here. But it is clear that those who are faithfully building on the foundation of Jesus Christ will receive a reward. And it is just as evident from Scripture, that the possibilities exist, that a person could live all his life as a child of God and not receive any reward. The apostle Paul wrote to the church at Corinth, speaking to believers:

> For no other foundation can anyone lay than that which is laid, which is Jesus Christ. Now if anyone builds on this foundation with gold, silver, precious stones, wood, hay, straw, each one's work will become clear; for the Day will declare it, because it will be revealed by fire; and the fire will test each one's work, of what sort it is. If anyone's work which he has built on it endures, he will receive a reward. If anyone's work is burned, he will suffer loss; but he himself will be saved, yet so through fire. (1 Cor. 3:11-15)

This passage makes it understandable that there is a judgment on the works of an individual believer, which will have some sort of impact on his future in the kingdom of heaven by receiving a reward or not receiving one. Some believe we will receive crowns as a reward and cast them at the feet of the Lord in worship (Rev. 4:10).

The Bible affirms that: "We shall all stand before the judgment seat of Christ" (Rom. 14:10). This again refers to all believers, not unbelievers. Misunderstanding the difference between reward and gift will cause confusion in understanding the coming judgments too. Sin has already been judged. The Lord Jesus by the grace of God "tasted death for everyone" (Heb. 2:9). He Himself is the "propitiation for our sins and not for ours only, but also for the whole world" (1 John 2:2). He is "the Lamb of God who takes away the sin of the world" (John 1:29). All sins, past, present, and future, of every person that has lived or will live have been dealt with through the death, burial, and resurrection of the Lord Jesus.

However, each person must make a personal choice to accept Him and His work to save them from the penalty of sin to receive the benefit. "Believe on the Lord Jesus Christ and you will be saved" (Acts 16:31).

Those who fail to believe in Him will receive the consequence of their decision. The Bible warns us that these will appear before the Lord at the great white throne. They will be judged, each one according to his works and end up being cast into the Lake of Fire. This is the second death also understood to be eternal death, separation from the Lord for all eternity (Rev. 20:11-15). They end up there because they failed to see their need and rejected God's gracious offer of everlasting life by faith alone in Jesus Christ alone. They go there because they don't have life, spiritual life that is eternal life.

Everyone is born into this life separated from God, born in the likeness of Adam. We are dead in our trespasses and sins (Eph. 2:1). In the Bible, death has the meaning of separation and is the absence of life; not physical life, but spiritual life. That's why Jesus told Nicodemus, "You must be born again" (John 3:3). He meant Nicodemus needed a spiritual birth to enter the kingdom of heaven. Otherwise, if one does not obtain spiritual life, he cannot enter. "He who has the Son has life; he who does not have the Son does not have life" (1 John 5:12). The only possibility then is the Lake of Fire, eternal death. That's the only alternative for the spiritually dead. People don't end up in the Lake of Fire because of their sin. They end up there because they don't have spiritual life. Jesus told the Jewish leadership, "But you are not willing to come to Me that you may have life" (John 5:40). That's the only way one receives this life: by believing on the Lord Jesus Christ. You don't work to get it or to keep it.

Everlasting life is a gift, not a reward for faithfulness. It is received the moment one is saved from the penalty of sin by believing the gospel. One sees a number of examples in Scripture that people are saved immediately upon believing. At the preaching of Peter on the Day of Pentecost, about three thousand souls were added (Acts 2:41). Not long after this, Peter, with John, preached again and about five thousand men believed (Acts 4:4). Peter, through a vision, was directed to go to Cornelius and his family, and they believed the gospel and the Holy Spirit came upon them. They spoke in tongues as evidence that the Gentiles were included in the salvation plan of God (Acts 10:43-45, 11:15-18). They were recipients immediately of everlasting life, but their reward would vary depending upon the faithfulness of their walk with the Lord throughout their life.

Walking by faith after one is saved is not automatic. It takes spiritual understanding and the will to be intentional to grow as a believer. Many think growing spiritually is inevitable. But building a relationship with God requires time and effort. It does not happen overnight. To learn to walk by faith, one must be in the Scriptures learning to apply those truths to one's life. "Faith comes by hearing, and hearing by the Word of God" (Rom. 10:17). It requires for-saking things in life to make time to be with God every day with the willingness to change to do life God's way rather than my way. "If anyone desires to come after Me, let him deny himself, and take up his cross and follow Me" (Matt. 16:24). The context here is dis-cipleship and reward: "For the Son of Man will come in the glory of His Father with His angels, and then He will reward each one according to his works" (Matt. 16:27).

Most of us were ignorant of the necessity to be in the Word as newborn babes in Christ. Many are not taught to get into the Word to grow as a functional and fruitful person as a child of God. So often a person such as this gets caught up going down the wrong road for a while in life. New believers usually try to live the new life in the power of the old nature. It can't be done and will only cause frustration and failure to do the things you want to do. That was the point of Paul to the Roman believers: "For what I am doing, I do not understand. For what I will to do, that I do not practice, but what I hate, that I do" (Rom. 7:15).

I remember this struggle myself; every day telling God, I would do better the next day and ended up doing the same thing. It wasn't until I realized from Scripture that you can't live an obedient Christian life in the strength of the old nature. I could only begin to live that way when I depended on the Spirit of God through the Word for the power and strength. You start to gain traction when you understand this principle. "I have been crucified with Christ; it is no longer I who live, but Christ who lives in me; and the life which I now live in the flesh I live by faith in the Son of God, who loved me and gave Himself for me" (Gal. 2:20).

A couple of friends told an account of witnessing to a coworker. The guy got saved. They bought him a Bible along with some other books to help him with word studies and general understanding. He began to read and study. One day after a while he came into work, threw all his books down in front of them, and said, "I quit!"

He meant he was done with pursuing the Christian faith. Why? Someone would say he probably was only a "professing" believer, that he was not a true convert. But I would say the likelihood was he became frustrated because of his lack of understanding of how to live the Christian life and just gave up. But that is precisely where God wants us. He wants us to give up trying and learn to simply trust in Him moment by moment, day by day.

That's why the apostle Paul in his epistle to the Roman church after eleven chapters exhorted them: "I beseech you, therefore, brethren, by the mercies of God, that you present your bodies a living sacrifice, holy acceptable to God, which is your reasonable service" (Rom. 12:1). Why would he urge believers to dedicate themselves in such a way? If spiritual growth and dedication were automatic, he would not have to beseech them to do so. But it is not automatic so we must be intentional to grow as a believer. If one fails to grow as a believer, their eternal destination is sure, but a reward might be lacking.

My curmudgeon buddy would ask how it's possible if all of our sin has been dealt with at the cross, then how can a believer be judged? Failing to do things out of faith is sin (Rom. 14:23). That's also a good question. I would answer it this way. When a believer is living carnally, simply living independent of God's direction, he or she is walking in darkness out of fellowship with God. The Holy Spirit is grieved and is unable to work in this person and through this person to accomplish the works that they should walk in. At this point, the Holy Spirit is trying to restore the believer back to fellowship. The result of their disobedient lifestyle bears no fruit for God. This lack of a fruitful walk results in loss of reward for such a person. So sinful living affects fellowship and lack of fellowship affects reward since one can only bear fruit when in fellowship.

There is a variety of views out there on how this reward business plays out when we get to heaven. My friend and I, from time to time, return to the subject because there is much about it in

Scripture that we don't fully understand. I'm not sure anyone has a complete handle on reward in the believer's life. We agree on that. We also agree on the fact that if someone is working only for the reward, then they're doing it for the wrong reason and likely in the wrong way.

I liked what one man said concerning rewards:

> The main point is that reward is completely distinct. Personally, I never worried whether I am doing things for the Lord "in the flesh" or "in the Spirit" — but that I am doing things for the Lord. As I began to grow in Christ and His Grace a couple of years after trusting in Jesus for my salvation, I began to realize that "the love of Christ constrains [motivates and compels] us" (2 Cor. 5:14a).[14]

The point of all this is to realize the gift of everlasting life is given freely to whosoever believes in His Son. Reward is dispensed by the Lord at the judgment seat of Christ upon the child of God who has been faithful, who has built on the foundation, Jesus Christ. The Lord told Abraham, "I am your shield, your exceedingly great reward" (Gen. 15:1). Don't live for the reward. Live for Him who gives the reward. Let God Himself be your motivation to live for Him. And then just rest in this truth: "Shall not the Judge of all the earth do right?" (Gen. 18:25).

---

[14] Jack Weaver, "Accursed or Innocent? Lordship "Salvation" Teacher", Expreacherman (blog) February 11, 2012, https://expreacherman.com/2012/02/11/accursed-or-innocent-lordship-salvation-teachers/#comment-11670.

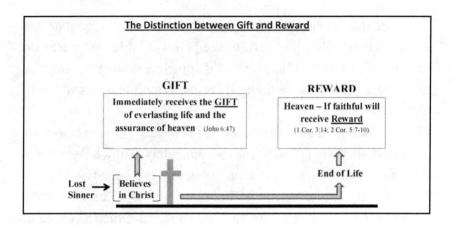

Chapter 11

Predestination

---

*A*re you predestined? The answer to that question is "yes", but probably not in the way that you think. There is prevalent teaching out there today that insists that you have no free will to choose to believe in God's good news. They reason that all people are totally depraved and have no ability to respond to God's message of salvation. So God had to predestine people to believe. And this predestination came before He created Adam and Eve. In other words, if people believe in Christ as Savior, it's because He chose to pick them from the beginning of creation to believe in Him. They were predestined to salvation and couldn't change it, even if they wanted to.

And on the other hand, those not predestined have no hope of a relationship with God and have zero chance of getting into heaven. For example, one popular commentary supports this view:

Scriptures indicates that no "free will" exists in man's nature, for man is enslaved to sin (total depravity) and unable to believe apart from God's empowerment. While "whosoever" may come to the Father, only those whom the Father gives the ability to will toward Him will actually come to Him. …those whom God

has chosen will believe because God has sovereignly determined that result from eternity past.[15]

This note is used to explain John 6:44: "No one can come to
Me unless the Father who sent Me draws him." I believe this is
a misunderstanding of this verse and unintentionally maligns the
character of God.

First of all, that verse is not speaking about predestination. It is
speaking of God drawing people to the Son. It is used here metaphorically of drawing by inward power, by divine impulse.[16] Jesus
also used the same word when He said, "And if I be lifted up from
the earth will draw *all peoples* to Myself " (John 12:32, emphasis
mine). The word "peoples" is added to the text for clarity, but I
don't think it's necessary. Jesus said He would draw all to Himself.
The point being in either 6:44 or 12:32, people are not being forced
to come, because not all come. But the Lord is drawing all because
He desires *all* men (people) to be saved and come to the knowledge
of the truth, for He gave Himself a ransom for *all* (1 Tim. 2:4, 6,
emphasis mine). But every individual must choose to respond to
the light that God gives. Jesus told the Jewish leaders, "I say these
things to you that you may be saved" (John 5:34). But He concluded about them: "But you are *not willing* to come to Me that
you may have life" (Matt. 5:40, emphasis mine). They would not
come to Him. Undoubtedly, this was an expression at that time of
their free will. God hadn't programmed them to unbelief. They
were Jewish, God's chosen people. But they refused to believe,
and God would hold them accountable one day if they remained
in their rejection of Him.

Secondly, John 6:44 doesn't say everyone that God draws
comes to Jesus. What it does mean is that no one can come unless

---

[15] MacArthur, The MacArthur Study Bible, 1592 [Note on John 6:44].

[16] Vine, Complete Expository Dictionary, 183 [New Testament].

the Father draws him. The Bible teaches us that God draws every person through the revelation of creation. Everyone should know there is a Creator by observing the miracles and intricacies around them.

For example, man cannot produce life from nonliving material. Life only comes from life. So where did life come from? The logical answer would be God:

What may be known of God is manifest [evident] in them, for God has shown it to them. For since the creation of this world His invisible attributes are clearly seen, being understood by the things that are made, even His eternal power and Godhead [Divine nature], so that they are without excuse. (Rom. 1:19-20)

People who reject Jesus because they buy into the evolutionary lie will one day be held accountable for their unbelief, not because He didn't choose them or predestine them. One's defense on Judgment Day will not be, "But God, you didn't pick me!" Their rejection will occur because they failed to make a personal decision to believe in Jesus as their personal Savior.

There are four passages in the New Testament that use the word "predestine." The Greek word for predestine is *proorizo* [προορίζω]. It means to mark out beforehand, to determine before.[17] It's translated four times as "predestine" or "predestined" in Romans 8:29-30, and in Ephesians 1:5 and 11. In each case, it refers to believers being predestined to something. However, as we will see, these four passages are not teaching that God predestines some to salvation and others to damnation.

In Romans 8:29-30, believers are predestined to be conformed to the image of Christ. The context speaks to glorification, the future state of a believer in heaven. The future glory will far outweigh the

---

[17] Vine, Complete Expository Dictionary, 165 [New Testament].

present suffering of believers (8:18). The whole creation eagerly waits for this, too (8:20). We also eagerly wait for the adoption to be complete; the redemption of our body (8:23). We are to wait for it with perseverance (8:25). All these things speak of our future glorification when we will be like Him (1 John 3:2). Those He predestined, He also glorified (8:30).

Who are predestined? Those He foreknew. Foreknow (Gk. *Proginosko*; πργινώσκω) means to know before. It's used in Acts of the Jews knowing Paul, "They *knew* me from the first" (26:5, emphasis mine). Here it is used of God knowing believers before or from the past. In the book of Galatians, the apostle writes at one point they did not know God: "But then, indeed when you did not know God, you served those things which by nature are not gods" (Gal. 4:8). But they came to know God and to be known by God: "But now after you have known God, or rather are known by God" (Gal. 4:9). This word for "know" in verse nine suggests relationship.[18] This definitely happened when they became believers. When they believed, God now *knew them* in a relational way. They became known by God. This is in opposition to those written about in the book of Matthew who did great and wonderful things in the name of Jesus, but He *"never knew"* them (Matt. 7:23).

When people believe on Christ as Savior they become known by Him—an everlasting relationship is established. Certainly God knows all people. But He doesn't have a relationship with all people. Only believers have a relationship with Him. Thus only believers are foreknown by God in such a way. The context of this foreknowing is not from the foundation of the world. It's not a reference to God choosing us before we were created. In the context, God is looking back to the moment unbelievers are justified by faith—the moment they trust Christ as Savior and come into a relationship

---

[18] Vine, Complete Expository Dictionary, 346 [New Testament].

with the Lord. At that point, God now knows the believers (Gal. 4:9). A relationship is established between them and God.

At this point, the believers in Rome had been saved from the penalty of sin and were foreknown by God. He knew them relationally from the day they believed. And those He foreknew He predestined (determined before) to be conformed to the image of Christ. This would speak to the certainty of their future glorification. This should have given them hope in suffering.

The third usage of "predestine" is in Ephesians 1:5. God predestined all believers to adoption into His family by Jesus Christ. We are adopted as children of God by faith in Jesus Christ. Our adoption will be complete at the redemption of our body when we are glorified (Rom. 8:23). God didn't have to adopt us to save us from the penalty of sin. However, He predetermined to begin the adoption the moment we believe. It's a significant positional truth that gives us full assurance that we are eternally secure. Just as we are children of human parents and nothing can ever change that, so we become God's children forever the moment we believe in Jesus Christ. And nothing can ever alter that relationship.

The last use of "predestine'" is in Ephesians 1:11: "In Him also we have obtained an inheritance, being predestined..." Believers are those "in Him" and are predestined to obtain an inheritance. This all happens after one is saved from the penalty of sin not before. And this is all God's doing, which He had determined beforehand to do, for those who would trust in Christ. He didn't predestine people to believe. *He predestined people who believe.* "In Him you also trusted, after you heard the word of truth, the gospel of your salvation; in Whom also, *having believed*, you were sealed with the Holy Spirit of Promise" (Eph. 1:13, emphasis mine).

These are the only four places in the New Testament that translate *proorizō* (προοριζω) as "predestined" or "predestine." Being predestined as suffering believers to be conformed to the image of Christ, to adoption into God's family, and to an inheritance should encourage the believer to endure. It should also give the believer assurance that nothing can separate him or her from the love of God (Rom. 8:39). None of these verses have anything to do with God predestining someone from eternity past to believe the gospel.

The reason some think this way is because they define total depravity as being incapable of exercising faith in Christ. This position is articulated in the following statement:

> We can never trust Christ for our salvation unless we first desire Him. This is why we said earlier that *regeneration precedes faith*. Without rebirth we have no desire for Christ. Without a desire for Christ we will never choose Christ. Therefore we conclude that before anyone ever will believe, before anyone can believe, God must first change the disposition of his heart.[19]

But does the Bible actually teach that? Does God make us believe? Are we born again before we're saved?

In the book of Ephesians, the Bible states we are dead in trespasses and sins (2:1). Proponents of this view reason, "How then can a dead person have the ability to believe?" If one uses this line of thought, a dead person can't do anything. But it's not speaking to being physically dead. It's speaking to people who are spiritually dead. As we have seen already, according to Romans 1, a spiritually dead person can respond to God through the revelation of creation. They can know that there is a creator and come to some understanding of his attributes and power. However, most do not respond in faith. They "suppress the truth in unrighteousness" (Rom. 1:18), not because they are incapable of exercising faith.

Anyone can also come to know the truth through the ministry of the Holy Spirit. Jesus said when the Spirit comes, "He will convict the world of sin, and of righteousness, and of judgment" (John

---

[19] R.C. Sproul, Chosen by God, (Wheaton, Illinois: Tyndale House Publishers, 1989), 118.

16:8). As I stated before, I have spoken to a lot of people over the last ten years at outreach events. I haven't found one that thinks he or she is perfect. All of them have acknowledged they do wrong things. Why? Because everyone has a conscience, and the Holy Spirit is convicting the world of sin. Moses Onwubbiko, founder of Grace Evangelistic Ministries aptly states: "He sent His Holy Spirit, whose work is to wake us up and cause us to see our hopelessness, to see our need for a Savior. In other words, the job of the Holy Spirit is to make the issue clear, to challenge our volition so we can make a clear choice for or against Christ."[20]

An unbeliever is not born again (regenerated) before they can believe. An unbeliever is regenerated the moment he or she believes. Jesus said, "He who hears My words and believes in Him who sent Me has everlasting life, and shall not come into judgment, but has passed from death to life" (John 5:24). Regeneration means you are given spiritual life. It's the Holy Spirit that gives life with a new nature, and that happens the moment a person believes the gospel: "having believed you were sealed with the Holy Spirit of promise" (Eph. 1:13). Unbelievers, dead in their trespasses and sins, are made alive at the moment of faith.

Examples of people in the Bible exhibiting free will began with Adam and Eve. They died spiritually the moment they decided to disobey God. Death in the Bible always speaks to separation, not the cessation of existence. At that moment, they experienced fear, guilt, and shame because of that separation. Their relationship with God died. So they went and hid from the Lord. They were dead to Him, but He came looking for them. He restored the relationship by promising them a deliverer who would crush the head of the serpent and clothed them with His righteousness. It was something they had not experienced before (Gen. 3:6-15, 21). Yet in their dead state, God went looking for them. And even in their spiritually dead

---

[20] Moses C. Onwubiko, James Faith without Works is Dead (Ontario: Essence Publishing), 160.

state, they still could respond to Him. They accepted the animal skins, His coverings for them—a picture of a substitutionary sacrifice. Why would He not do the same for us?

Jesus had ministered to the people of Israel for three years. Not long before His death, He laments over Jerusalem for their refusal to believe in Him: "O Jerusalem, Jerusalem, the one who kills the prophets and stones those who are sent to her! How often I wanted to gather your children together, as a hen gathers her chicks, but you were *not willing*" (Matt. 23:37, emphasis mine). They were God's chosen people! But because of their continued willing rejection of the Lord, judgment would come upon Jerusalem. Why would Jesus lament over people that He knew were not predestined to believe, if that were the case? Would that not have been a disingenuous show of emotion and concern almost to the point of being deceitful?

Obviously, Jesus had great concern out of His love for them, not because they could not believe, but because *they would not believe*.

The apostle Paul "reasoned in the synagogue every Sabbath, and persuaded both Jews and Gentiles" (Acts 18:4). Later in his ministry, "some were persuaded by the things which were spoken, and some disbelieved" (Acts 28:24). Here the apostle is trying to bring about a change in their mind by convincing them of the truth. Why would he try to persuade anyone, if all people have been predestined?

As you can see from these examples, depravity cannot mean that humans have no ability to respond to God. It merely means a spiritually dead man is incapable of providing a way out of his sinful condition. Humans are incapable of restoring their relationship with God. God had to intervene, or we would have no hope.

Everyone comes into this world with a fallen nature passed down from Adam (Rom. 5:12). We are all separated from God at birth. And there is nothing we can do to change it. We are condemned sinners helpless to restore our relationship with God. What we need is spiritual life and forgiveness.

That's why God sent His Son. Jesus died for the sins of the whole world: "For God so loved *the world* that He gave His only begotten son that *whoever believes* in Him should not perish but have everlasting life" (John 3:16, emphasis mine). He died for everyone: "He by the grace of God should taste death *for everyone*" (Heb. 2:9, emphasis mine). "He entered the most holy place *once for all* having obtained eternal redemption" (Heb. 9:12, emphasis mine). That's why God commands *all men* everywhere to repent (to have a change of mind about Christ) (Acts 17:30), because everyone has the capacity to respond to the revelation that God has given them. That's the only way a just God, who provided a solution for sin for everyone, can hold people accountable for their unbelief.

Of course, some will argue God is sovereign. I certainly do not disagree with that. But God's sovereignty is infinitely powerful and intelligent enough to allow humans to have a free will, isn't it? "There are many plans in a man's heart, nevertheless the Lord's counsel – that will stand" (Prov. 19:21). And how could God predestine some and not others, and still be true to His word? The Lord said He "did not send His Son into the world to condemn the world, but that the world through Him might be saved" (John 3:17). How could God be truthful by saying He doesn't want the world (the people) condemned, knowing that most will be condemned, not because they won't believe, but because He didn't predestine them to believe? Once again, He would be disingenuous in His concern. It just doesn't fit the character of a loving, gracious, merciful, faithful, truthful, and just God.

Predestination is definitely a biblical doctrine. But some have changed it to fit their philosophy that a man cannot believe unless God regenerates and predestines him. That principle violates numerous Scriptures and is not what is taught in His Word. It makes God out to be an unjust judge by sending people into a Godless eternity by holding them accountable for what they could not do.

One person said it this way: "this god created billions of vessels of wrath fitted for destruction—commanded them to do what he had willed them unable to do—then sent them to Hell for not doing it. If this is your god, you have my sympathy."[21]

Are you predestined? You are. If you have trusted in the Lord Jesus Christ as Savior, then you are predestined for heaven. If you haven't, you are predestined for the Lake of Fire. If you're headed for the Lake of Fire, you can change that today. Believe on the Lord Jesus Christ, and you will be saved and be predestined for heaven.

Predestination of the Believer

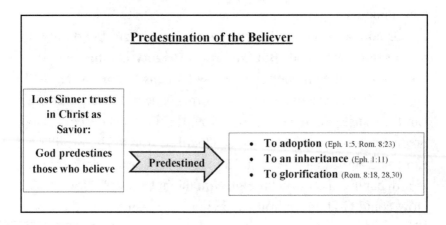

Predestination of the Believer		
Lost Sinner trusts in Christ as Savior: God predestines those who believe	**Predestined**	• **To adoption** (Eph. 1:5, Rom. 8:23) • **To an inheritance** (Eph. 1:11) • **To glorification** (Rom. 8:18, 28,30)

---

[21] Unknown source

Chapter 12

Perseverance

—◦⟨⟨⟩⟩◦—

*I*n the last chapter, we saw how the biblical doctrine of predestination is twisted to make it something it is not. In this chapter, we will see how many Bible teachers do the same thing to the doctrine of perseverance. They make it out to be something inevitably a saved person will do, not something a saved person should be encouraged to do. Theologian RC Sproul explains this popular view:

> Writing to the Philippians, Paul says, "He who has begun a good work in you will perfect it to the end" (Phil. 1:6). Therein is the promise of God that what He starts in our souls, He intends to finish. So the old axiom in Reformed theology about the perseverance of the saints is this: If you have it—that is, if you have genuine faith and are in a state of saving grace—you will never lose it. If you lose it, you never had it.[22]

William MacDonald, in the *Believer's Bible Commentary*, comments on 1 John 2:19 in an attempt to explain all true believers persevere to the end:

---

[22] R.C. Sproul, "Tulip and Reformed Theology: Perseverance of the Saints," Ligonier Ministries (blog), April 22, 2017, www.ligonier.org/blog/tulip-and-reformed-theology-perseverance-saints/.

"They went out from us, but they were not of us; for if they had been of us they would have continued with us; but they went out that they might be made manifest, that none of them were of us"(I John 2:19). Here we learn that true faith always has the quality of permanence. If a man has really been born again, he will go on for the Lord. It does not mean that we are saved by enduring to the end, but rather that those who endure to the end are really saved.[23]

These kinds of statements by credentialed men only confuse the message of salvation. It makes it a works driven salvation and causes you to look at your personal performance. If I am performing well, or if I am a good boy or girl, then I feel good about going to heaven. However, the opposite is also true. If I'm not good, then I have no assurance and will begin to question my salvation based on this teaching. These men may mean well, but their interpretation methodology is flawed.

Understanding Philippians 1:6

The apostle Paul was thankful for their "*fellowship* in the gospel from the first day until now [At the time he wrote to them]" (Phil. 1:5, emphasis mine). The good work in verse six is singular. It is a good work that the entire Philippian church participated in. Paul was confident that God would complete that work in them until the day of Jesus Christ. Most assume it is speaking to salvation, but the good work in the context of the letter refers to their assistance in helping Paul in the spreading of the gospel.

How did they assist Paul in the gospel? In the beginning of his ministry of the gospel, they shared with him by providing for his necessities when he departed from Macedonia (Phil. 4:15-16). They continued to share with him a number of times after he departed

---

[23] William MacDonald, *Believer's Bible Commentary* (Thomas Nelson Publishers, 1995), 2314.

Macedonia: "No church *shared* with me concerning giving and receiving, but you only; for even in Thessalonica you sent aid once and again for my necessities" (Phil. 4:16, emphasis mine). They "shared" with him is the same word used for "fellowship" in 1:5. In chapter one, the noun form is used. In chapter four, the verb form is used.[24] The two words connect the thought of fellowship by sharing in something together.

They had supported Paul so that he could spend more of his time preaching the gospel. We do that even today by supporting missionaries. Both the giver and the missionary are "striving together for the faith of the gospel" (Phil. 1:27). Because they gave to Paul for his needs, he didn't have to devote that time to work, allowing him more time to preach the gospel. Paul sarcastically wrote to the Corinthian church that he robbed other churches to preach the gospel to them (2 Cor. 11:8-9). This good work (giving to the gospel ministry) that God started in them would not be complete until the Day of Jesus Christ. In other words, the result of their giving to the ministry of the gospel would impact generation after generation, until the day of Jesus Christ.

This verse does not support the idea that all believers will persevere in faith and obedience. But people use this and other verses out of context to support their view of perseverance.

Understanding John 2:19

The apostle John was writing to a group of believers concerning those who were trying to deceive them (1 John 2:26). Because he was writing to them, he was not present with them. So when he said these antichrists went out from us, the "us" could not be speaking to him and to whom he was writing. It seems better to understand "us" from chapter one concerning John and those who had seen Jesus before and after His resurrection—"that which we have seen

---

[24] Vine, Complete Expository Dictionary, 115, 233 [New Testament].

and heard we declare to you, that you also may have fellowship with *us*" (1 John 1:3, emphasis mine) Here the "us" is about John and others who had the privilege of literally seeing and hearing Jesus, possibly a reference to the other apostles.

John is warning them about many antichrists in the world (1 John 2:19).These antichrists denied that Jesus is the Christ (1 John 2:22). They departed from John and his companions and made it clear that they were not with John. Is this verse teaching that anyone who drifts away from going to church or from truth is unsaved? Is this teaching that these didn't persevere? No. It is teaching that those who left were unsaved, because they rejected the truth that Jesus is the Christ, not because they didn't persevere in faith. They needed to be wary of those who teach such heresy. To see this as "professing" believers who prove they are not "true" believers by not persevering is reading that into this verse.

There are other verses that are used to say all "true" Christians will persevere. We will look at some of the more popular ones. But before moving on, let's remember justification, being delivered from the penalty of sin, occurs immediately at the point of belief in Jesus as Savior. It's simply trusting in the Person and work of Christ. In John chapter three, Jesus explained to Nicodemus how simple it was to be delivered from the penalty of sin, by using an illustration from the Old Testament. This illustration would have been familiar to him: "As Moses lifted up the serpent in the wilderness, even so must the Son of Man be lifted up, that whoever believes in Him should not perish but have eternal life" (John 3:14-15).

Moses led the people around the land of Edom. They had refused to enter into the Promised Land because of unbelief (Heb. 3:19). For that reason, God would take them on a forty-year journey to discipline them. The men who refused to go into the land, who were twenty years or older, would die in the wilderness during those forty years. And as they journeyed once again, they complained they should have remained in Egypt. Because of all their complaining, "The Lord sent fiery serpents among the people, and they bit the people, and many of the people of Israel died" (Num. 21:5-6). So the people confessed they had sinned and asked Moses to intercede for them. He did, and God gave them a solution.

Then the Lord said to Moses, "Make a fiery serpent and set it on a pole; and it shall be that everyone who is bitten, when he looks at it, shall live" (Num. 21:8). If anybody was bitten and looked to the pole, he lived (Num. 21:9).

God didn't remove the serpents, but He provided the only way for them to survive the bite. They merely had to believe Him and by faith look to the pole. One look and they were healed. The pole was lifted up so all could see it. It was their choice to look or not.

Jesus used this illustration to explain to Nicodemus how a person could live forever by looking in faith to Him, "lifted up." Jesus explained later when he said, "If I am *lifted up* from the earth, I will draw *all peoples* to myself. This He said, signifying by what death He would die" (John 12:32-33, emphasis mine). That's how simple God made salvation from the penalty of sin. If one looked to the pole when bitten, that person was immediately healed. He did not die. Similarly, when someone looks in faith to Jesus and His substitutionary death on the cross, he or she is immediately saved from sin's bite, eternal death. He or she will never perish, never die spiritually, because the believing sinner receives everlasting life at the moment of faith in Christ.

A person doesn't have to persevere to the end of life to get saved from sin's penalty. But one does have to persevere to be delivered from the power of sin; the everyday struggles that come our way as a child of God. Remember you have two natures. "The flesh lusts against the Spirit, and the Spirit against the flesh and these are contrary to one another so that you do not do the things that you wish" (Gal. 5:17). Your old nature can keep you from persevering in the moments of time and circumstances of life, so that you never grow to maturity and you never bear any fruit. We will see that principle next in the parable of the sower.

Understanding the Parable of the Sower (Matt.13:3-23; Mark 4:3-20; Luke 5-15)

Those who think that all "true" believers persevere, see this parable representing two types of people: saved, represented by the last soil, and unsaved, represented by the other three soils. According to them, the second and third soils represent unsaved people because they fail to persevere. But the parable is not about perseverance; it's about responses to the Word of God. "When anyone hears the Word of the kingdom" (Matt. 13:19), it will provoke four possible reactions.

The first soil definitely represents those who reject the word of the kingdom. "Those by the wayside are the ones who hear, then the devil comes and takes away the word out of their hearts, *lest they should believe and be saved*" (Luke 8:12, emphasis mine).

The second soil is stony ground. Life manifests itself—it sprang up immediately (Mark 4:5). The word is received with joy. They "*believe* for a while and in time of temptation fall away" (Luke 8:13, emphasis mine). Matthew says they stumble when tribulation or persecution arises, because of the word (Matt. 13:21). They are in the kingdom when they believed (justified), but tribulation or persecution prevents them from enduring.

The epistle to the Hebrews demonstrates this type of believer (Heb. 5:11-12, 10:32-36). They had "endured a great struggle with sufferings." And they knew they had a "better and enduring possession" in heaven (Heb. 10:32, 34). But they needed to endure again (Heb. 10:36).

There is reason to believe they were under persecution and contemplating a return to following the Mosaic Law. Did they endure? No one knows for sure. But it's clear from the word that they had a possession in heaven, whether they endured or not. The writer wasn't encouraging them to persevere so that they would get to heaven. He wanted them to persevere to receive a great reward, and in doing so, bring glory to God (Heb. 10:35).

The third soil is thorny ground. The thorns sprang up with the seeds and choked them out (Luke 8:7). "The cares of the world and the deceitfulness of riches choke the Word and he *becomes unfruitful*" (Matt. 13:22, emphasis mine). Luke says these "are choked with cares, riches, and pleasures of life, and bring no fruit to maturity" (Luke 8:14). They bring no fruit to maturity. To become unfruitful, they must have initially bore a little fruit. Remember only saved people can bear fruit. They respond to the word by failing to persevere and become unfruitful.

Demas is an example of such a believer. He served with Paul as a fellow laborer but later forsook him, "having loved this present world" (Philem. 24; 2 Tim. 4:10; Col. 4:14). Paul was in prison or under house arrest. Christians were being persecuted. Demas possibly departed out of fear of being imprisoned himself. Would that mean he was unsaved? No, he was just not willing to persevere through some difficult times.

Another example is Timothy. The apostle Paul had no one who would sincerely care for the Philippians church except Timothy. "For all seek their own, not the things which are of Christ Jesus" (Phil. 2:21). The only available faithful disciple around Paul was Timothy. All the other disciples looked out for their own interests. Was Timothy the only one saved or the only faithful disciple at that time? Paul merely said Timothy was the only disciple he could trust to minister to them faithfully. Timothy had "proven character" because he served with Paul in the gospel (Phil. 2:22).

And of course, the fourth soil represents saved people who respond faithfully to the Word. They *"bear fruit with patience* [endurance]" (Luke 8:15, emphasis mine). The Christian life is not a sprint. It's a marathon, and it takes endurance in the Christian life to bear fruit.

There were quite a few people in the Bible who did not persevere in faith and obedience. Back in chapter six, we saw how Solomon failed to persevere. The entire nation of Israel came out of Egypt under the blood of the lambs, a picture of justification. "By faith they passed through the Red Sea as by dry ground" (Heb. 11:29). They were walking by faith, a picture of sanctification. But then they failed to go into the Promised Land, because of unbelief (Heb. 3:19). They were fearful of the giants. They weren't persevering.

Although believers can fail to persevere and produce no fruit (2 Pet. 1:8, 9), the point of the parable is not whether they are saved or not. The point of the parable is that Jesus taught His disciples, who would eventually go out to sow the Word of the kingdom, that they could expect different types of responses to it. The first one does not believe and has no potential of bearing fruit. They reject the Word of the kingdom. The second and third soils represent those who believe for a while but fail to persevere, which results in little or no fruit. The last soil is those that bear much fruit. Implied is that fruitfulness would require keeping His word, endurance amidst trials and persecution, and self-denial of chasing after the things in the world. This should have encouraged them to remain faithful, when they saw no fruit or when they came up against persecution as they often did.

We should have the same perspective. We should expect some people to reject the message, some to fall away due to tribulation and the cares of the world, and some to bear fruit. This should not defeat us nor discourage us. We should strive to be the ones who "having heard the word with a noble and good heart, keep it and bear fruit with patience" (Mark 4:15). We should remain faithful to Him and His Word despite the consequences or the results. And we can only do this by exercising our faith, depending on the power of the Spirit through the understanding and encouragement of God's Word for the strength to endure.

When I started to pray for a greater understanding of His grace, my thinking began to change concerning perseverance. Scriptures that confused me before slowly began to become clearer. God taught me something about Himself. I challenge you to ask God to give you a deeper understanding of His grace. You might be amazed!

One of the first things He brought to mind was the fact that no one can define what it means to persevere to the end. What does that look like? From man's point of view, we can only see the outward things that a person does. We can't see the heart, the mind, and will. We can't see the struggles or the turmoil that gurgle up inside. I always find it interesting that most of those who believe one must persevere to the end, still allow for periods of life for falling away. But, they will say a "true" believer will always return to the faith.

One proponent of perseverance wrote, "Although saving faith may have lapses; it always has the quality of permanence."[25] When I read statements like this, I wonder, "How long can the lapse be? Can it be a year? Two years? Five years? How long does a lapse have to be until a person proves he's not truly saved?" No one can answer these questions. What if someone fell into a lapse in their Christian faith for a year or two and died? What if another fell into a lapse for a year or two, and then got back on track in the Christian walk? Did the one go to hell, because he fell away for a while, and died before he got back on track? Was one only a "professing" believer while the other was a "true" believer?

These folks use the word "true" believer a lot. What's a "true believer" supposed to look like? Judas looked like a "true" believer and disciple. When Jesus said to His disciples that one of them would betray Him, they had no clue who it was: "The disciples looked at one another, perplexed about whom He spoke" (John

---

[25] MacDonald, Believer's Bible Commentary, 1294.

13:22). That's because Judas acted no differently than them—at least what they observed outwardly.

I am aware Jesus said there would be tares and that both would be reaped at the same time. A tare looks like wheat, but it is a weed. There are indeed people who appear to know Jesus, that aren't saved. They go to church and do all the religious things. For that reason, they may look like a Christian, but they never understood, or they never believed the gospel. They're not tares because they believed the gospel but failed to persevere. In fact, if they failed to persevere, they likely wouldn't be in the church. Tares are ones who think religious duty, like going to church, baptism, communion, and praying, are ways to please God. But these are works that can be done in the flesh. Things of this nature could never take away your sin and give you spiritual life. Tares are people who never believed the gospel.

Perseverance doesn't prove anything about a person in regards to their salvation from the penalty of sin. Both believers and unbelievers can look the same in the church and outside the church. For example, let's say that an elderly lady in the neighborhood lost her husband. Two other neighbors get together and decide to help her by cutting her grass. One of the men, a Christian, decides to help her because of his faith. He understands that love for God should manifest itself in loving your neighbor. He sees his assistance as being obedient to the faith to help someone in need. The other fellow is an agnostic and wants to help her as well. He has always enjoyed doing things for others because it is what he believes you should do and it makes him feel good. A third neighbor observes the grass cutting throughout the summer. Can he determine the faith of these two individuals? No. It would be impossible because we cannot see into another person's heart.

What if your neighbor, a Christian and an elder in his church, had an adulterous affair with a coworker's wife? He gets her pregnant and tries to figure out a way to get rid of the husband. One day you observe police cars at his home. Shortly thereafter, the police escort him out of the house in handcuffs. They arrest him for conspiracy to commit murder. He is found guilty and is sentenced to forty years. What would you think? No way possible that he was a real believer. King David ordered Uriah, one of his elite warriors, to be killed. The king did this to cover up his adulterous affair with Uriah's wife. And he was a man after God's own heart (Acts 13:22)!

I'm not writing this to encourage anyone to do anything of the kind. The consequence of one bad choice can be disastrous. It can ruin your life and the lives of others. "The fear of the Lord prolongs days, but the years of the wicked will be shortened" (Prov. 10:27). God may discipline you severely (Acts 5:1-10; James 5:19-20). My point is simply that you and I cannot identify a believer based upon their good or bad performance. Sin can have serious and significant consequences. That's why the Bible instructs us to "keep your heart with all diligence, for out of it springs the issues of life" (Prov. 4:23). If we're not careful, we can fall into grave sin as a believer. But the truth is that we can't determine a person's salvation based upon outward behaviors.

Some believers persevere, and some do not. To persevere, we must be surrendered to the Spirit of God through the Word of God, depending on Him for the strength, day by day and moment by moment. "You will keep in perfect peace, whose mind is stayed on You, because he trusts in You" (Isa. 26:3). That's the principle application for perseverance.

Understanding 2 Corinthians 5:17

The advocates of perseverance like to use 2 Corinthians 5:17. "Therefore if anyone is in Christ he is a new creation; old things have passed away; behold all things have become new." The MacArthur commentary says: "After a person is regenerate, old value systems, priorities, beliefs, and plans are gone. Evil and sin are still present, but the believer sees them in a new perspective and they no longer control him."[26]

It's unrealistic to think that a new believer will no longer be controlled by sin. You might as well discard much of the New Testament, especially the books of 1 Corinthians and James. There would be no need to instruct the church to put off the old man and to put on the new man.

David Anderson, in his book, *Bewitched: the Rise of Neo-Galatianism*, tells of a college friend who was promiscuous and got saved. But he continued in his promiscuity for several months. After a few months, he was convicted by Christ and turned from that sin. He explains:

> But for some time after receiving Christ, it would be hard for another human being to see any change in his life. ...The point though is that the fruit was working inside him before anything was externally visible. That young man could have hardened himself to the Spirit and continued in promiscuity and experienced self-destruction and loss of inheritance. But his justification and indwelling by the Spirit took place prior to any change in behavior.[27]

This verse is speaking to positional truth. "In Christ", a believer has a new position. He is a new creation no longer "in Adam." His new position is "in Christ" with a new nature. However, God doesn't remove the old nature. In his new position, the believer possesses both the new and the old (sin) nature.

This verse indicates a huge spiritual change has occurred in a person who is born again. But this verse never guarantees a believer cannot be controlled by the flesh, the sin nature. It is evident from

---

[26] MacArthur, The MacArthur Study Bible, 1771.

[27] Anderson, Bewitched, 207.

the Bible that believers can struggle with sin, and life experience confirms this. This is not to say a child of God should accept this as normal. But if one thinks this verse guarantees transformation and perseverance, he will soon be defeated and disappointed.

Understanding 2 Corinthians 13:5

At one time, I used this verse out of context. "Examine yourselves as to whether you are in the faith." In other words, make sure you are persevering as evidence you are a "true" believer. A fellow brother in the Lord told me that he tells his adult children this. But, how many times do you have to examine yourself to conclude you are indeed in the kingdom? It seems to me that a better solution would be to have a conversation about the Lord. In doing so, it would be easier to know what they have trusted to save from the penalty of sin. If they have placed their faith in the person and work of Christ, then it would be better to reassure them that they are saved, because Jesus says they are. "Most assuredly, I say to you, he who believes in Me has everlasting life" (John 6:47).

When well-meaning folks tell others to examine themselves, they are only training them to look at their works (religious activity) and behavior. This results in only two possibilities. I am in because I think I'm a good person, or I am not because I'm not living righteously enough. It leads to the road of self-righteousness or the road of despair. In my case, it could have led me to despair, except that I weaved through all the erroneous teaching by comparing it to God's Word. In the end, examining your works doesn't get to the heart of the issue. When it comes to being delivered from the penalty of sin, has one believed on the Lord Jesus Christ? That is the issue.

No one is ever told in Scripture to look at your works to determine whether you're saved or not. (Not even in the book of James as we will see in Chapter 14.) It may be good for believers to do so to determine whether they are in fellowship with the Lord. Do I need to confess some sinful way and forsake it, to be delivered from the power of sin, so that I am glorifying God with my life and have his hand of blessing on me? That should be a continual practice, but not to determine whether one is saved or not from the penalty of sin.

So what does this verse mean? Well, first of all, trying to understand any verse out of context will usually lead you to a wrong understanding. The background here is that the Corinthian church questioned the proof of Christ speaking in the apostle (2 Cor. 13:3). In the three chapters before this, he is defending his apostleship (10-12). He appeals to the signs of a true apostle that were accomplished among them, "in signs and wonders and mighty deeds" (2 Cor. 12:12).

Back in chapter three, he wrote they were "an epistle of Christ, ministered by us, written not with ink but by the Spirit of God, not on tablets of stone but on tablets of flesh, that is, the heart" (v. 3). From this you can see the apostle is not questioning the sincerity of their salvation. However, they questioned his authority to speak on behalf of Christ: "since you seek a proof of Christ speaking in me" (2 Cor. 13:3).

He tells them to examine themselves to see whether they were in the faith. If they answer yes, then they are the proof that Christ is speaking in the apostle, because Christ saved them through Paul's ministry of the gospel (Acts 18:1-11). Thomas Stegall points out, according to the grammar of the verse, Paul assumes the Corinthians are *not* "disqualified," but are truly "in the faith" and "Christ is in [them]."[28] In other words, the apostle expected them to respond positively that they were in the faith. Thus, ironically by affirming they were saved, they were also affirming the truth and proof that Christ was speaking in the apostle.

---

[28] Thomas Stegall, "Is 2 Corinthians 13:5 A Warning to False Professors?," Grace Family Journal, July 3, 2018, https://www.gracegospelpress.org/is-2-corinthians-135-a-warning-to-false-professors/

Understanding Matthew 24:13

This is another verse that is often used to say "true" believers will endure to the end. "But he who endures to the end shall be saved." Again, context must be king. This passage is speaking to the future tribulation, the end of the age (Matt. 24:3, 6). Jesus is speaking to his Jewish disciples about the future kingdom, in regards to the Jewish people and the nation of Israel. The Old Testament makes it evident that the Lord saves Jerusalem and Israel from total annihilation (Zech. 12:2-9, 14:4; Isa. 11:11-12; Jer. 30:7). Those who endure this horrible time to the end of the tribulation will have their physical life saved and enter into the millennial kingdom, the thousand year reign of Christ on Earth (Rev. 20:2-6). Nine verses later, Jesus makes it clear that "unless those days were shortened no flesh would be saved" (Matt. 24:22). Again this is a reference to the inevitable fact that no one would survive physically if those days were not shortened. It's not speaking to enduring to be saved from the penalty of sin. That doesn't fit the biblical context of the passage or the requirement of the gospel.

Understanding Colossians 1:23

This is another verse that is used to prove that a "genuine" believer will persevere: "if indeed you continue in the faith, grounded and steadfast, and are not moved away from the hope of the gospel which you heard."

The apostle prayed for them, that they "would walk worthy of the Lord, fully pleasing Him, being fruitful in every good work and increasing in the knowledge of God" (v. 10). He prayed for them to mature in their faith. His goal was to "present every man perfect in Christ Jesus" (v. 28). Perfect does not mean sinless. It's a reference to spiritual maturity.

But they would have to continue in the faith and not move away from the gospel, in order for that to happen. If they do not persevere in the faith, they will not mature. That's the point of verse 23. This verse is speaking to their sanctification, not justification.

Did the Apostle Paul Believe in Perseverance to be Saved from the Penalty of Sin?

In many of his epistles to the churches, the apostle Paul writes knowing there is the possibility that they could fail to persevere. Specifically, he was concerned about them being deceived into believing false doctrines or experiencing tribulation that would lead to departing from the faith. To the church at Thessalonica, he wrote, "For this reason, when I could no longer endure it, I sent to know your faith, lest by some means the tempter had tempted you and our labor might be in vain" (1 Thess. 3:5). They began as followers of the Lord (1 Thess. 1:6). But, the apostle had concerns the disciple-making ministry that he had begun with them might have been in vain if they had abandoned the faith. He sent to them to see if they had continued in their faith in Christ. He was concerned about their sanctification, not their justification.

In regards to the Galatian believers, he was concerned because they were being bewitched and turning away from the one who called them to a different gospel (1:6). His concern for them is expressed in chapter four verse nine: "But now after you have known God, or rather are known by God, how is it that you turn again to the weak and beggarly elements, to which you desire again to be in bondage?" They were believers on the brink of going in the wrong direction and not persevering in faith in Christ.

To the Ephesian church, he explained the purpose for the equipping of the saints was so they would not be "tossed to and fro and carried about with every wind of doctrine by the trickery of men in the cunning craftiness of deceitful plotting" (4:14). They could become confused, and so can we if we don't stay strong in the Lord and the power of His might. To do this, we must "put on the whole armor of God, that you may be able to stand against the wiles of the devil" (Eph. 6:11). The devil targets the believers to make us dysfunctional and unfruitful as children of God so that we won't persevere in the truth.

To the Colossian church, he was concerned "lest anyone should deceive you with persuasive words" (Col. 2:4). He warned them to beware of false teachers that were in major doctrinal error who would try to "cheat [take captive] you through philosophy and empty deceit" and "not according to Christ" (Col. 2:8). He was concerned for the false teachings out there that could cause them to drift away from their faith in Christ. They would fail to mature (Col. 1:28).

One last example is Paul's first letter to Timothy.

And having food and clothing, with these we shall be content. But those who desire to be rich fall into temptation and a snare, and into many foolish and harmful lusts which drown men in destruction and perdition. For the love of money is a root of all kinds of evil, for which some have *strayed from the faith* in their greediness, and pierced themselves through with many sorrows...(1 Tim. 6:8-10, emphasis mine)

The love of money can cause believers to stray from the faith. That was the point of the third soil in the parable: they "are choked with cares, riches, and pleasures of life, and bring no fruit to maturity" (Luke 8:14). Riches tempt believers so that they become dysfunctional and unfruitful. He wrote to caution Timothy, a believer, of such temptation: "But you, O man of God, flee these things" (1 Tim. 6:11).

It's abundantly evident that the apostle, writing God-inspired Scripture, did not believe a child of God would inevitably persevere to the end of life in faith. He wrote to them to encourage and exhort them to be faithful among the false teachings and tribulations that came their way, so their life would glorify God, and they would not be useless and unfruitful as a child of God.

Failing to persevere in faith can bring some significant consequences. It may cause you to lack assurance of heaven. I know of a couple that had experienced a loss of a family relationship because of a misunderstanding. Several years later, they attempted to reestablish the relationship. They were rejected by the other family member. Fellowship was never restored. God is not like that. He wants to restore us back to fellowship. But, the choice is ours. "Draw near to God and He will draw near to you" (James 4:7).

There are other verses also that get distorted to mean a "true" believer will persevere to the end. Learn to understand the context of Scripture so that you won't be misled. "True" believers get saved by faith in Christ and immediately have everlasting life. That's the only type of believer there is. However, not every Christian disciple perseveres and matures spiritually. But God desires us to persevere and to grow. And we should.

> Therefore gird up the loins of your mind, be sober, and rest your hope fully upon the grace that is to be brought to you at the revelation of Jesus Christ; as obedient children, not conforming yourselves to the former lusts, as in your ignorance, but as He who called you is holy, you also be holy in all your conduct, because it is written, "Be holy, for I am holy." (1 Pet. 1:13-15)

Believer and Perseverance

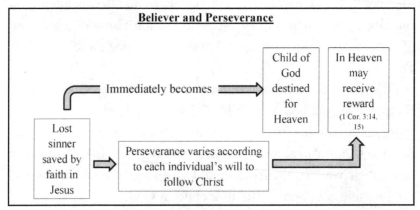

Believer and Perseverance

Lost sinner saved by faith in Jesus ⟹ Perseverance varies according to each individual's will to follow Christ

Immediately becomes ⟹ Child of God destined for Heaven ⟹ In Heaven may receive reward (1 Cor. 3:14, 15)

Chapter 13

Falling Away from the Faith

————⟶∘⟨⟨⟩⟩∘⟵————

We looked at this in the last chapter on perseverance. Of course those who say only "true" believers persevere, and also teach that it's impossible for "true" believers to fall away. "Falling away" and "failure to persevere" mean basically the same thing. Most who say it's impossible to fall away will also acknowledge salvation is permanent and cannot be lost. But if a person falls away, they were never truly saved, according to them; they were only "professing" believers or "false" believers. They have all kinds of adjectives that describe the faith of someone who falls away. Adjectives that are not found in the Scriptures like: false, spurious, non-saving, non-genuine, dead (meaning never existing), apparent (that does not save), counterfeit, and imitation. More recently, I came across a new term, "phenomenological", to describe them.

How does anyone know then that they have the right kind of faith that saves you? You persevere in faith, that's how. If you still have faith at the end of your life, then you had "saving" faith. Do you see the circular reasoning in their way of understanding salvation? You could never know you are going to heaven until you get to the end of your life.

Who can fall away from the faith? Some believe a saved person can fall away and lose their salvation. Others believe only people who are almost saved can fall away. But falling away from the faith can only happen to believers, as they are the only ones in a relationship with God. You can't fall away from a relationship that doesn't exist. Hebrews 6 is usually the go-to chapter to prove that one can fall away from the faith.

Hebrews 6: 4-6

This may be one of the most misunderstood passages in the entire New Testament. It's misunderstood because many people assume it is impossible for "true" believers to fall away from the faith. But the Bible doesn't teach that.

> For it is impossible for those who were once enlightened, and have tasted the heavenly gift, and have become partakers of the Holy Spirit, and have tasted the good word of God and the powers of the age to come, if they fall away, to renew them again to repentance, since they crucify again for themselves the Son of God, and put Him to an open shame. (Heb. 6: 4-6)

There are generally three views on these verses:
1. These are saved people who lose their salvation.
2. These are people who experience the truth, reject it, and then never can get saved.
3. These are saved people who fall away, but remain saved.

The problem with the first view is that this verse says they cannot be renewed to repentance. So if you lose it, you can never get it back. This is not consistent with the grace of God that is taught in the Bible.

The second view is also not consistent with the grace of God. For example, King Manasseh rejected truth most of his life. He did more evil than any other king of Judah. He reigned for fifty-five years. He would not listen to the Lord. He acted more wickedly than the godless Amorites (2 Kings 21:11). So God brought judgment against him, and he was imprisoned in Babylon. There he humbled himself and cried out to God. God heard his prayer and brought him back to Jerusalem (2 Chron. 33:1-16). At the end of his life, Manasseh became a man that knew the Lord. If God extended grace to Manasseh, then anyone can be saved.

In addition, the second view is shown to be incorrect by at least three of the five descriptive phrases in this passage. These phrases describe people who are saved. They were enlightened. It's the same word used in chapter 10, verse 32 of Hebrews for "illuminated." In the past, they had endured a great struggle after they were illuminated. They endured the struggle, knowing they had an "enduring possession in heaven" (Heb. 10:34). "Enlighten" and "illuminated" is the same word in Greek, addressing the same group of people. They can't possess heaven in chapter ten, and not possess it in chapter six.

They also tasted three things: the heavenly gift, the Word of God, and the powers of the age to come. In Hebrews 2:9, Jesus tasted death for everyone. Taste is used metaphorically of experience. These people experienced the heavenly gift, the gift of everlasting life (Rom. 6:23). In the gospel of John, Jesus spoke of living water (metaphorically of everlasting life) as the gift of God (4:10-14). This would imply that regeneration had taken place. How could they experience spiritual life (everlasting life) apart from being born again?

They were partakers of the Holy Spirit, as well. They were the same people described as beloved brethren and partakers of the holy calling (Heb. 3:1). The word "partaker" has the idea of sharing in, partaking of.[29] From this, it should be reasonable to conclude they had the indwelling of the Spirit.

At the least, being enlightened, experiencing the heavenly gift, and being partakers of the Holy Spirit describe a person that is in a

---

[29] Vine, Complete Expository Dictionary, 201, 318 [New Testament].

relationship with the Lord through faith in Jesus Christ. How could a person be enlightened, experience the heavenly gift, the good word of God, the powers of the age to come, and be partakers of the Holy Spirit, and not be saved?

These believers were on the brink of falling away from faith in Christ. An unbeliever cannot fall away from a relationship that he or she doesn't have. Only believers are in relationship with God. Thus, only believers can fall away from the faith. The gift of everlasting life begins at the moment of faith and continues in an everlasting home in heaven. Once you are saved you cannot lose it. If one could lose everlasting life, it would not be everlasting life. It would be a temporary life. The Lord in His word said to the same people, "I will never leave you nor forsake you" (Heb. 13:5). I choose to believe God over man.

The book of Hebrews was written to Jewish Christians experiencing tribulation, possibly persecution from their fellow countrymen. At the time they were likely living in Jerusalem. The easiest route for them to avoid trouble would be for them to revert back to Judaism, to depart from their faith in Christ.

But why would it be impossible to renew them to repentance? In other words, what could prevent them (believers) from being restored to fellowship with God? (All believers have a relationship with God, but all are not in fellowship with Him) Restoration to fellowship always requires repentance. Also, what does it mean to "crucify again for themselves the Son of God and put Him to open shame"?

First of all, "renew" must mean they had repented. They did. When they trusted in Christ, they repented of dead works (the religious rituals of the Law) and received eternal life (Heb. 6:1). But as children of God, they had become dull of hearing spiritual truth (Heb. 5:12). If they returned to Judaism they would lose fellowship with God, but not their relationship.

Secondly, the animal coverings that God provided for Adam and Eve pictured the future death of Christ. All of the Old Testament blood sacrifices pointed to the death of the One [Jesus] who would take away the sins of the world. His sacrifice would be once for all (Heb. 9:12). If they reverted back to Judaism, their involvement in sacrificing animals would have suggested that His death did not take away sin. Their participation in the Law would have falsely depicted that the Messiah and His death were still in the future. This would put Him to open shame, since He had already come "and put away sin by the sacrifice of Himself" (Heb. 9:26). Therefore, it would be impossible to renew them to repentance [to restore them to fellowship] while they chose to remain in Judaism, because Jesus would not be crucified a second time. "He entered the Most Holy Place once for all, having obtained eternal redemption" (Heb. 9:12).

The writer of Hebrews warned this body of believers about drifting away from so great a salvation (Heb. 2:1-3). They had become dull of hearing spiritual truth and should have been teachers. But they needed to be taught the first principles of the oracles of God again (Heb. 5:11-12). In other words, they had retrogressed in their spiritual walk and were being warned of the potential of putting Christ to open shame by returning to the sacrificial system. He will warn them in chapter ten of the consequence of sinning willfully in this manner.

In verse nine, the writer speaks about the things that accompany salvation. What should accompany salvation: works prepared for us that we should walk in them (Eph. 2:10), godly living (Titus 2:12), and growing in the grace of the knowledge of Lord and Savior Jesus Christ (2 Pet. 3:18). If they return to the Old Testament law of sacrifices and rituals (dead works), they will be barren and unfruitful in the knowledge of our Lord Jesus Christ. And since God wants us to be fruitful, the Holy Spirit warns them not to fall away. They needed to go on to maturity by faithfully enduring the trials. In doing so, it would glorify God and be good for them.

Understanding Hebrews 10:26-31

This is an additional warning in the book of Hebrews. And it's a scary one at best.

> For if we sin willfully after we have received the knowledge of the truth, there no longer remains a sacrifice for sins, but a certain fearful expectation of judgment, and fiery indignation which will devour the adversaries. Anyone who has rejected Moses' law dies without mercy on the testimony of two or three witnesses. Of how much worse punishment, do you suppose, will he be thought worthy who has trampled the Son of God underfoot, counted the blood of the covenant by which he was sanctified a common thing, and insulted the Spirit of grace? For we know Him who said, "Vengeance is Mine, I will repay," says the Lord. And again, "The LORD will judge His people." It is a fearful thing to fall into the hands of the living God.

These verses have caused some to doubt their salvation because they know they have willfully sinned. Others say these verses, along with the other warnings, show they should question their salvation, because they probably are not saved. They are apostates, having never truly believed in Christ. They would say Judas is an example of such a person.[30]

Verse 26 can create fear when it speaks of willful sin. But who does not sin willfully after being saved from the penalty of sin? Is not all sin willful in that a person is responsible for his or her actions and thoughts? So what is the writer trying to communicate?

---

[30] McDonald, Believer's Bible Commentary, 2192 [note on 10:26].

If you come to a difficult passage, understand the context and the fact that the gospel is a free gift; that it doesn't guarantee perseverance and believers can fall away; then these difficult verses become a little easier to understand.

Because they are Jewish, the willful sin is likely a reference to the Old Testament. A person who defiantly despised the word of the Lord was to be executed, "cut off from among the people" (Num. 15:30). The example of such a sin was a man who had collected firewood on the Sabbath. No work was to be done, and he willfully and knowingly violated the command. (Num. 15:32-36) No sacrifice would stop God from judging that sinner. He would physically die (the most severe type of temporal judgment). But his early death did not mean that he didn't go to be with the Lord.

The Willful Sin

What was the willful sin that they considered? They were tempted to abandon their faith and return to the Old Testament sacrificial system. "Let us hold fast the confession of our hope without wavering, for He who promised is faithful" (Heb. 10:23). The writer warns them to hold fast to their faith in Christ. He has already explained the law could "never with these same sacrifices, which they offer continually year by year, make those who approach perfect. For it is impossible that the blood of bulls and goats could take away sins" (Heb. 10:1, 4). The writer is making the point that Jesus' sacrifice is far better than those of animals. Don't waver in your faith and go back to Judaism. This would not have been said to them unless they contemplated a move backward.

By going back to the sacrificial system, they will abandon their confession of faith in Christ. If they do there is a certain expectation of judgment and fiery indignation, which will devour the adversaries. Some see this as eternal separation from God in the Lake of Fire (hell). But is this to be understood in this light?

So far in this chapter, the writer has addressed these people as believers. In verse 20, he calls them "brethren." He includes himself as having the potential for departing when he wrote in verse 22, "let *us* draw near;" in verse 23, "let *us* hold fast;" and in verse 24, "let *us* consider one another." In verse 26, he again includes himself: "if *we* sin willfully." He doesn't say "you" as though he was immune from the possibility. And his audience has not changed.

Judgment and Fiery Indignation

So you might be thinking, "How does judgment and fiery indignation, which will devour the adversary (unbeliever), come upon a believer since we are no longer under the penalty of God for sin?"

First, these Jewish believers contemplated leaving Christ to return to Judaism. "Therefore let us go forth to Him, *outside the camp*, bearing His reproach" (Heb. 13:13, emphasis mine). The "camp" here is a reference to Judaism. The city of Jerusalem was to the Jews what the camp in the wilderness had been to the Israelites.[31] The Jews placed great significance on Jerusalem. To them, it was the city of the great king (Ps. 48:2). They would take oaths swearing by Jerusalem (Matt. 5:34-35). If they failed to go outside the camp, they would at the least return to Jerusalem or were already living there. But for them, they were to understand there is no "continuing city, but we seek the one to come" (Heb. 13:14). They were to seek the New Jerusalem, "whose builder and maker is God" (Heb. 11:10).

If they return to Judaism, they put themselves in jeopardy of experiencing God's judgment in the following way. Toward the end of Jesus' ministry, He pronounced judgment on Jerusalem and the temple. When the disciples brought to His attention the building and the temple, He told them that they would be destroyed: "not one stone shall be left here upon another" (Matt. 23:37–24:2). He

---

[31] Vine, Complete Expository Dictionary, 38 [New Testament].

108

warned them that when they saw Jerusalem surrounded by armies, they should flee to the mountains. This would indicate that her desolation was near. He said this would be "the days of vengeance, that all things which are written may be fulfilled" (Luke 21:20-22). He foretold that this destruction would come upon that generation because they did not recognize the day of their visitation (Luke 19:41-44).

Historically, this is indeed what happened. Eusebius, who served as bishop of Caesarea in the third century, recorded that Jews who became believers in Jesus fled the city during the siege by the Romans and survived. Many Jews who stayed in Jerusalem were killed. God's judgment on them had fallen.[32] This judgment could well be the judgment and fiery indignation which would devour the adversaries spoken about in Hebrews 10. The book of Hebrews was written in the late 60s AD. This destruction took place in 70 AD. In God's grace, He warned them to avoid falling away to protect them from a worse fate in the near future.

If these believers were to go back to Jerusalem, they could expect physical harm in this coming judgment, which was intended for those Jews who had rejected Jesus as the Messiah. In other words, the judgment was not meant for them, but they could fall victim to it by reverting back to Judaism. God would not supernaturally protect them from harm, for they had already been warned about going back to the sacrificial system.

Consider Lot as an example. The angels had to persuade and lead him by the hand out of Sodom. Second Peter 2 makes it clear he was saved (v. 7). What if he had refused to leave, like his sons-in-law? Would God have withheld judgment against Sodom, because Lot was still there? Certainly not! He would have destroyed the city if Lot refused to leave. He would have died in the judgment that was not intended for him. He would have fallen

---

[32] Renald Showers, Spiritual Gifts (Published by Renald Showers, 2007), 53.

in the judgment and fiery indignation that God intended for the adversaries in Sodom.

These Hebrew Christians were similarly risking the same kind of fate if they returned to Judaism. If a person were to do this, would you think he was deserving of worse punishment? If a person under the law dies on the testimony of two or three witnesses, how much worse would it be if such a person trampled the Son of God underfoot, counted His blood by which he was sanctified a common thing, and insulted the Spirit of grace? The natural desire for justice in us would agree that such a person would be deserving of a worse punishment. Not that they would receive a worse punishment, but that they would *"be thought worthy"* of a worse punishment.

Such a believer who would go back to the old covenant law would by his action insult the Spirit of grace. In essence, by his actions, he would be scorning the Son's sacrifice and counting the blood by which he was sanctified a common thing; in other words, equal to that of an animal sacrifice. He would be saved by grace, but then go back to the sacrificial system of law! Like those in the Galatian church, they would have fallen from grace (Gal. 5:4)..

Summary of Hebrews 10:26-31

Vengeance is God's prerogative, and He will repay. Vengeance proceeds out of justice, not out of a sense of vindictiveness like a human would respond. His vengeance would ultimately fall on that generation of Jewish people for their rejection of Jesus Christ as foretold by Him. He would judge them, although it had not yet happened at the time this epistle was written. It is a fearful thing to fall into the hands of the living God. There would be only a fearful expectation of judgment and fiery indignation intended for God's adversaries.

That's why the writer tells them to remember the former days when they "endured a great struggle with sufferings… knowing that you have a better and enduring possession for yourselves in heaven" (Heb. 10:32, 34). They already possessed heaven by faith in Christ. They were warned and reminded of what they already possessed. They could not lose the possession of heaven, but they could lose rewards and suffer earthly consequences if they follow through with their willful sin.

Suffering Shipwreck in Your Faith

If one is not careful, you can shipwreck your faith. In Paul's first epistle to Timothy, he wrote about a couple of men who fell away: "*concerning the faith have suffered shipwreck* of whom Hymenaeus and Alexander, who I delivered to Satan that they may learn not to blaspheme" (1 Tim. 1:18-20, emphasis mine).

Here the Bible speaks of two men who suffered shipwreck in their faith. He didn't say they weren't "true" believers or that their faith was "false" or "non-genuine." He said they suffered ship-wreck. To suffer shipwreck, you have to be on the ship. So what did the apostle do? He treated them as believers and brought disciplinary action against them so that they would learn not to blaspheme. He had instructed the church at Corinth not to judge those outside the church because God will judge them. They were to judge those inside: "anyone named a brother" (1 Cor. 5:11-13). That is what the apostle did in this case.

He guarded the flock by turning them over to Satan. This is the same thing he instructed the Corinthian church in dealing with a serious sinning brother (1 Cor. 5:5). Some believe this means to excommunicate one from the fellowship by handing them over to the world system, which is Satan's realm. Whatever this meant, it was action to be taken against a brother or sister in the faith who was in a severe type of sin.

Hymenaeus was mentioned again in Paul's second letter to Timothy along with a guy named Philetus. He told Timothy that they had strayed from the faith by "saying the resurrection is already

111

past; and they overthrow the faith of some" (2 Tim. 2:18). Some suggest these people did not have genuine faith, because genuine saving faith cannot be overthrown.[33] But you can't have anything overthrown that you don't have. How can a country be overthrown, if the country doesn't exist?

In the same way, how could a person have their faith overthrown, if they didn't have faith to begin with? That opinion doesn't hold water. These people had faith. Their faith was being upset by those who were teaching that the resurrection of the dead was passed.

Summary

I think it's evident from Scripture that only a believer can fall away from the faith in various ways. Unbelievers can't fall away from something they don't possess. Jesus even rebuked his disciples several times for having little or no faith (Matt. 6:30, 16:8; Mark 4:40). Believers get frustrated and give up. Sometimes believers get fed up with the church. It may make them unfruitful, but it doesn't make them unsaved.

Can a believer fall away? Yes, they can. Many believers fall away at least for a period of time during their life. The trouble is that we cannot be sure of their identity. People come to church for a time, make a profession of faith, and then disappear. Were they saved? Who can know other than God? We can only go on what a person tells us.

But trying to make the case that no believer can ever fall away or fail to persevere, is twisting Scripture to say something that it does not. That's the purpose for discipleship and fellowship so that when someone falls, somebody is there to help him back up. We don't walk away saying he or she was never saved. But it's their decision if they want the hand to help them back up.

---

[33] MacArthur, The MacArthur Study Bible, 1878 [note on 2:18].

All believers are susceptible to falling away. When things get tough, the easy way out is to quit. I know there have been a few times when I just wanted to go live on a mountainside. No, I wasn't going to sacrifice animals, but I would have lived a self-directed life, not a God-directed one. "A man who isolates himself seeks his own desires; he rages against all wise judgment" (Prov. 18:1). And if I would have done that, lived in the mountains, after a while I may have become a nature worshipper. That is how drifting and departing from the faith happens. It doesn't "un-save" you. It simply causes one to be useless as a child of God. You choose to serve your own interests and desires. You fail to glorify God with your life, and it won't be good for you. It's not the life God desires for us.

Joshua posed a question to the Israelites when they were in the Promised Land.

And if it seems evil to you to serve the Lord, choose for yourselves this day whom you will serve, whether the gods which your fathers served that were on the other side of the River, or the gods of the Amorites, in whose land you dwell. But as for me and my house, we will serve the Lord. (Josh. 24:15)

And to believers today, he could ask similarly, "Who will you choose to serve: yourself or the Lord?"

If you have trusted Jesus as your Savior, you have a choice to follow Him or to follow the dictates of your old nature. It's a choice you have to make each day, moment by moment. A lack of faithfulness doesn't un-save you, but it keeps you dysfunctional and unfruitful as His child.

Only Believers can Fall Away**

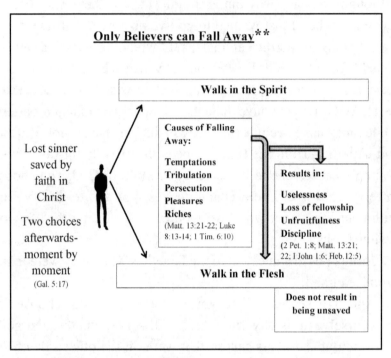

**Only those who have a relationship can fall away. Unbelievers have no relationship with God. You can't fall away from something you do not have.

Chapter 14

Faith Without Works is Dead

"Thus also faith by itself, if it does not have works, is dead" (James 2:17). There you have it. If you are not showing forth works, then you are not saved. At least that's what many will tell you today. For them, this is the acid test to tell if someone is a genuine believer if you have works. It perverts the gospel, if you think through what they are saying. Some will quote John Calvin who supposedly wrote, "We are saved by faith alone, but not by a faith that is alone." That makes no sense. First Corinthians 3:13-15 makes it clear that a person can be saved apart from having done any works.

The modern-day study Bible has become popular for the average person in the pew. There's a lot of useful information in them to help those of us who find some of the Bible difficult. The apostle Peter even comments about some of Paul's writings, "in which are some things hard to understand, which unstable people twist to their own destruction, as they do the rest of the Scriptures" (2 Pet. 3:16). But generally what happens over time is that believers hold the commentary equal to the Scripture. But commentaries are written by man.

For example, when it comes to this verse in James, I researched thirty-two commentaries and study Bibles. Twenty-seven of them taught that this verse in James shows that works are proof of salvation; that if there are no works, there is no salvation. Two of the commentaries were at best confusing. And only three said it spoke to believers who did not express their faith in good works.

A long time ago, a pastor encouraged me to remember, "Who says the crowd's right?" Just because a majority says something doesn't mean it's correct. Typically the crowd isn't right. So does one judge an explanation of a passage based on the majority view? No. Any passage is to be understood in light of the context of the Scriptures.

I believe this majority interpretation has done more harm to Christianity than almost any other verse in the Bible. I say that because it makes one look to their personal performance for assurance and not to the Lord Jesus Christ. That's a recipe for not growing, for not producing any good works by faith, and for causing doubt. As stated before, looking to your performance as proof of salvation will do one of two things. It will cause you to lack any assurance causing anxiety and fear, or it will make you self-righteous. The Spirit of God ministers to us to convict us of things that we should change. How can I change and grow if I have a self-righteous attitude about myself? Or how can I mature as a believer, if I'm fearful and anxious, because I can't believe God accepts me? You can't.

There is no way one can grow in the grace and knowledge of the Lord until you have a solid understanding that it is the Lord Jesus Christ who has saved you from the penalty of sin by trusting in Him alone through faith alone. "For by grace you have been saved through faith, and that not of yourselves, it's the gift of God, not of works lest anyone should boast" (Eph. 2:8-9). *You will never have full assurance until you understand you have complete for-giveness.* Your deliverance from the penalty of sin, eternal death, is guaranteed the moment you believe the gospel.

So as we look at this passage, we need to look at it in this light. James is writing to Jewish believers who are scattered abroad because of Christian persecution (James 1:1-2). In his epistle, he calls them "brethren" or "beloved brethren" fifteen times. He exhorts them to "be doers of the word and not hearers only, deceiving themselves" (James 1:22). If one does not become "a forgetful hearer but a doer of the work, this one will be blessed in what he does" (James 1:25). James is exhorting them to be doers and be blessed. He's not saying if you do not work, you will not make it to heaven! What he is saying is you won't be blessed.

In chapter two, he calls them brethren and instructs them not to show partiality in their faith by paying attention to the rich and dismissing the poorer brother (James 2:1-4). Then he lays out an example of their lack of properly applying their faith. "If a brother or sister is naked and destitute of daily food, and one of you says to them, 'Depart in peace, be warmed, and filled', but do not give them the things which are needed for the body, what does it profit?" (James 2:15-16)

What are some observations about these two verses?

- In his example, he is speaking about believers, "if a brother or sister."
- The believer does not meet the need of another believer.
- A lack of a faith response does not help the one in need.
- He implies they were not profitable by their attitudes toward one another.

James concludes, "Even so faith, if it hath not works is dead, *being alone*" (James 2:17, KJV, emphasis mine). The King James Version makes it clear that faith is "alone." In other words, it doesn't say faith does not exist. In the example used in James, it's by itself having no works because the believer doesn't respond by helping another brother in physical need. If something is "alone", it must still exist or be present.

Secondly, people err when using words like "saving" faith. I realize it can describe the difference between justification and sanctification (walking by faith). But, those who use "saving" faith here imply there is another type of faith that doesn't save. The Bible uses words to describe faith like: "little" faith, "great" faith, "full" of faith, "no" faith, and a faith that is "dead." It never uses the combination "saving faith." Concerning deliverance from the penalty of sin, a saved person initially exercised faith. An unsaved person never exercised faith. These people were already saved from the penalty of sin as previously demonstrated. They were not walking by faith. They were believers sitting in the middle chair. They were not being delivered from the power of sin. They had a relationship with God, but they were out of fellowship with Him. They were living carnally, similar to the church at Corinth (1 Cor. 3:1-4).

Thirdly, the word for dead, *nekros* (νεκρός), does not mean false or non-existent. In Romans 6:11, it refers to the ideal spiritual condition of believers regarding sin, "dead to sin." In Revelation 3:1, it refers to a church that is inactive and barren: "but you are dead."[34] It means useless, inactive.

In the Bible, physical death refers to the separation of the soul from the body. So James aptly compares faith that is dead to a body that is dead (James 2:26). A body that is dead still exists as a body, but it is separated from the soul. It ceases to perform its intended function. A dead body becomes useless, of no profit. Likewise, faith is useless (dead metaphorically) when it produces no works. They were not doers of the word, only hearing it, thus deceiving themselves (James 1:22).

Fourth, James explains this kind of response does not profit the person in need which is the purpose of good works. Paul writes to Titus concerning good works, "This is a faithful saying, and these things I want to affirm constantly, that those who have believed in God *should* be careful to maintain good works. *These things are good and profitable to men*" (Titus 3:8, emphasis mine). He also instructs, "And let our people also learn to maintain good works,

---

[34] Vine, Complete Expository Dictionary, 148 [New Testament].

to meet urgent needs, that they may not be *unfruitful*" (Titus 3:13, emphasis mine). In the KJV and NKJV, "should" is used when speaking about good works (Eph. 2:10; Titus 3:8). Good works are not necessarily a natural response of those who have been delivered from the penalty of sin. All believers need to learn and maintain good works. They should be fruitful. But the possibility exists that if a believer is not taught, he may be unfruitful, but saved.

Interestingly, also, is what the apostle doesn't say about good works. He doesn't say that good works are profitable to prove one is saved or that they are a guaranteed result of salvation. In fact, only a few verses back in Titus 3, he makes the point that we are not "saved by works of righteousness which we have done" (Titus 3:5). The apostle Paul is instructing Titus to teach believers that they should do good works because those things help others and they will be fruitful in doing so. In other words, maintaining good works will mean that their faith will be productive, not dead (useless).

Understanding James 2:14

But some will ask, "what about verse 14?"

"What does it profit, my brethren, if someone says he has faith but does not have works? Can faith save him?" (James 2:14)

James inferred, "No, faith cannot save him." But what does the question mean? Is it referring to the deliverance from the penalty of sin? Or is it speaking to the deliverance from the power of sin in the life of a believer?

Since he is writing to believers to correct them concerning various sinful practices, it should be evident that he is speaking to the latter. They needed to be delivered from the power of sin. In chapter 1:21, he told them that the implanted word could save their souls from all filthiness and the overflow of wickedness. Yes, that's right. They, as believers, could participate in such a lifestyle. In actuality, they were involved in a great deal of wickedness (James 4:1-5, 11, 16, 5:19). The phrase "save your soul" likely was understood to mean "to save the life."[35]Hearing and doing the implanted word would deliver them from the power of sin and possibly from premature physical death (James 1:15, 5:19). That seems to be the best interpretation of the context–in the book of James. He's not saying that people who have no works are unsaved.

Just in a practical sense, judging your works or the works of another is a pretty tricky thing to do. What is doing a good work? From James' example, helping a brother or sister in need would be a good work. The problem here is that any number of unsaved will readily lend a hand to someone in need. Unbelievers give to charities, do charitable work, etc. They can look the same outwardly as a believer. Good works are not quantifiable. How many are necessary? Who can judge whether you are doing works? Even believers can do good works for the wrong reason. If I think I must "show" good works to prove to myself that I am saved, then my old nature will work hard to do those things to assure me. I will produce good works in the flesh rather than in the Spirit. I will focus on myself and not on Christ. I will be a worker rather than a worshipper. Worshippers can work as well. But they'll do it with the proper motivation of loving God by serving others. "Beloved, if God so loved us, we also ought to love one another" (1 John 4:11). It's the difference between a have-to life and a want-to life. "Serve the Lord with gladness" not because you have to, but because you want to (Ps. 100:2).

Understanding James 2:19

Some, propose there are those who believe but aren't saved, use the demons in verse 19 as an example. "You believe there is one God. You do well. Even the demons believe and tremble" (James 2:19). Based on this, they will tell you that it's more than

---

[35] Zane Hodges, James, The Grace New Testament Commentary, (Denton: Grace Evangelical Society 2010), 1109.

believing that saves you. Demons believe, and they end up in the Lake of Fire.

The problem with that application is that demons cannot be saved by the blood of Christ. Their fate is sealed. They know God exists. They were in heaven with him until they rebelled with Satan.

The meaning here is that even the demons have a right doctrine about God and it causes them to tremble. The demons know the truth that God is one. Because of what they know to be true, they tremble. Their belief elicits a response from them. The point is that if the belief of demons manifests itself, so shouldn't the life of a believer manifest itself in a way that results in good works? Is it not reasonable to expect that a child of God should express his or her faith in good works?

To show a faith that is working correctly, one that is living, not dead, James gives the illustration of two people, Abraham and Rahab. They were both justified by faith for salvation from the penalty of sin apart from works (Rom. 4:5). That is an unseen transaction that occurs with God when one believes the gospel. But here James says they are justified by their works to demonstrate to others that they were people of faith.

Abraham (James 2:21-24)

When it comes to Abraham, his faith had matured to the point that he was willing to sacrifice his son at God's command (Heb. 11:19). Think about it. If you had a son, would you be willing to sacrifice him at God's command? Did it take such a great act of faith to prove that Abraham was saved? Or did it demonstrate that his faith had matured?

According to James, Abraham's faith was working together with his works, and his faith was perfected or made mature (James 2:22). He had come into a faith relationship with God many years before this (Gen. 15:6). But his obedience to the command revealed he was trusting in God to fulfill His promise even if he sacrificed Isaac.

121

He concluded God could raise him from the dead (Heb. 11:19). The first time Abraham was justified before God. The second time he is justified before man that he was a doer of the word; that he was willing to do whatever God commanded. Abraham showed man his faithfulness to God, and because he followed through with this great act of faith, he has the awesome privilege of being called "the friend" of God (Isa. 41:8). King Jehoshaphat acknowledged to God that Abraham is "your friend forever" (2 Chron. 20:7).

Rahab (James 2:25)

Rahab, like Abraham, demonstrated her faith when she received the messengers and sent them out another way. She had believed in the Lord God of Israel (Josh. 2:12). After that "By faith the harlot Rahab did not perish with those who did not believe, when she hid the spies with peace" (Heb. 11:31). She demonstrated her faith to them by hiding the spies and sending them out another way. She committed treason to justify her faith before them. Her work of concealing the spies justified her before men. Her faith produced action that was helpful to Israel's army.

She also saved her life as a result of acting in faith. She is an example to these Jewish New Testament believers that living faith versus a dead faith may keep you physically alive (James 2:17, 5:20). This should have resonated with the audience that received this letter.

What a blessing—a Gentile harlot included in the Jewish lineage of the Messiah! She was blessed for her faithfulness. And so would James' audience be blessed, if they obeyed by being a doer of the word (James 1:25).

In Summary

Failure to walk by faith as a believer will result in a number of negative consequences. A constant lack of faithfulness and obedience to the Word of God will result in a ruined life that is lacking in fruitfulness and good works. Peter exhorted believers to add to faith: virtue, knowledge, self-control, perseverance, godliness, brotherly kindness, and love (2 Pet. 1:5-7). Without the development of these qualities, one can be barren and unfruitful (2 Pet. 1:8). Even to the point that he has forgotten that he was cleansed from his old sins (2 Pet. 1:9)!

Secondly, one risks the possibility of discipline from the Lord. "For who the Lord loves He chastens" (Heb. 12:6). Many in the Corinthian church had become weak, sick, and died. The Lord had chastened them for their disobedience (2 Cor. 11:30, 32). Believers cannot continually mistreat one another with impunity. At some point, God will intervene.

Faith without works is dead. This was written to believers, "to the brethren." Failing to understand the book of James is written to believers can lead one into a host of spiritual pitfalls. You'll become a worker apart from being a worshipper. You cannot grow in your relationship with God, even though you may do a host of religious activities at your church and in your community. And you may develop a judgmental attitude toward other believers by relegating them to merely "professing" believers. Or it may tank your walk because you will not have the assurance of salvation since you can never know if you have done enough. And lastly, you will misunderstand the purpose: to exhort those who are saved to a vibrant living faith. You will fail to see any application in your life. Then you will not learn from their failures, so you can experience the abundant life that the Lord desires for all believers and in doing so glorify Him.

Good Works are not Automatic

Ephesians 2:10	We are created in Christ Jesus for good works that we should walk in them.
1 Timothy 5:10	Widows over sixty were provided for if they were well reported for good works.
1 Timothy 6:18	The richer brethren were exhorted to be rich in good works.
Titus 3:8	Believers should be careful to maintain good works.
Titus 3:14	Believers must learn to maintain good works.
Hebrews 10:24	Let us consider one another in order to stir up good works.

- Good works result when a believer abides in Christ, being controlled by the Spirit of God through the Word of God (Rom. 8:6; Gal. 5:16).
- Only the Lord can see the motivation of the heart. He knows the difference between works motivated by the flesh and ones motivated by the Spirit. "And there is no creature hidden from his sight, but all things are naked and open to the eyes of Him to whom we must give account" (Heb. 4:13).
- "If anyone's work is burned, he will suffer loss; but he himself will be saved, yet so as through fire" (1 Cor. 3:15). There is the potential that a saved person's works can be burned if the works are not built on the foundation of Jesus Christ.

Chapter 15

Saved by Grace

<hr />

*B*ack in Chapter Three, we saw the gospel is an offer to "whosoever" believes in Jesus for everlasting life. Man can do absolutely nothing to earn it. It is all of God's provision for us if one is willing to accept it by faith. But the difficult part is to believe there is nothing one needs to do to receive it and keep it. Because of pride, people find it hard to believe salvation from the penalty of sin is a gift that only needs to be received by faith alone. Adding to the pride issue, people have the wrong understanding of who God is as well.

I remember my dad telling me about a story when he was a child in the late 1920s. He was one of eleven children, the third oldest. They had a large family Bible that sat on a table in one of the rooms. This Bible had pictures of angels and spiritual warfare. He said they would open it up to those pictures and then they would scatter like chickens with fear. Sometimes I think many of us start this way in the Christian life. We have a wrong fear of God. Indeed fear of hell is a good thing. But when we get saved, we continue to carry that same mental image of this wrathful God who is going to send us to hell for misbehaving. And frankly, I think this understanding of God has caused many to lack assurance. Some of these folks make you focus on your behavior and not on the Savior.

I do not deny the holiness of God and that He will one day execute His wrath. I also realize many others have focused entirely on God's love ignoring His other attributes. Personally, the fear of God made me see my need for God's love, mercy, and grace. All of us have difficulty understanding how God's character attributes like His holiness, love, justice, mercy, and grace, work together in complete harmony. We tend to focus on one and ignore the others. Some wrongly over emphasize His wrath, while others His love. But if you are a believer, I can confidently say you should "gird up the loins of your mind and be sober-minded, and rest your hope fully upon the grace that is to be brought to you at the revelation of Jesus Christ" (1 Pet. 1:13).

Look unto Jesus the author and finisher of our faith (Heb. 12:2). Jesus is full of grace and truth (John 1:14). Grace and truth are interwoven like a two strand rope. You can't have the one without the other. Grace does not dismiss the other attributes of God. But grace is what we need to properly apply the truth in our lives and toward the lives of others. If we did not understand the truth that God is holy, it would be impossible to understand His grace. If God's love simply accepted man in His fallen state, He wouldn't be holy. The truth about God and His attributes helps us to understand the grace, mercy, and love of God to greater and greater depths.

Some also fail in other ways in understanding the person of God. They think He is like us. But He is infinitely distinct from us: "You thought that I was altogether like you" (Ps. 50:21). "'For My thoughts are not your thoughts, nor are your ways My ways,' says the Lord. 'As the heavens are higher than the earth so are My ways higher than your ways, and My thoughts than your thoughts'" (Isa. 55:8-9). He is infinite in power, and His understanding is unsearchable (Ps. 145:3). He calls things into existence from nothing. He said, "Let there be light and there was light" (Gen. 1:3). "By the word of the Lord the heavens were made; and all the host of them by the breath of His mouth" (Ps. 33:6). "Let all the earth fear the

Lord; let all the inhabitants of the world stand in awe of Him. For He spoke, and it was done; He commanded, and it stood fast" (Ps. 33:8). How is it then that we think of Him being only a little above us? He's not the man upstairs. And He's not my co-pilot.

Our biggest problem with God is His holiness. "It is a fearful thing to fall into the hands of the living God" (Heb. 10:31). When God came down on the mountain at the giving of the Ten Commandments, in thunder and lightning and smoke, and the mountain was shaking, the people feared for their lives. Afterward, the people told Moses, "You speak to us, and we will hear, but let not God speak with us, lest we die" (Exod. 20:19). Can you imagine being there, witnessing the effect of God's presence on that mountain? They weren't calling Him "the man upstairs" on that day.

Later when Moses wanted to see God, the Lord told Moses, "You cannot see My face; for no man can see Me and live" (Exod. 33:20). Samson's father, after an encounter with the Angel of the Lord, thought they would die, "because we have seen God" (Judg. 13:22). The Lord dwells in unapproachable light, who no man has seen or can see (1 Tim. 6:16). God's holiness is a huge problem for us. Just one "small" sin is an infinite offense to Him because He is holy.

So where does that leave us? Well we, if that were His only character trait, would be doomed as doomed could be. But thank God, He is also loving, merciful, gracious, and kind! "The Lord is gracious and full of compassion, slow to anger and great in mercy" (Ps. 145:8). "But You, O Lord, are a God full of compassion, and gracious, longsuffering, and abundant in mercy and truth" (Ps. 86:15). If He were not, no one would have a chance.

In fact, His first response to the first act of disobedience was mercy and grace. Mercy is not giving what is deserved. His mercy was evident. They didn't die. Grace is giving what is not deserved. In His grace toward Adam and Eve, He gave them what they did not deserve. They deserved to be separated from Him forever. But in

His grace, He went looking for them, not because He didn't know where they were, but because they were hiding from Him. He did not have to seek them out. They did not deserve that. But that's what He did because He cared for them. He responded in grace for that is who He is.

He then provided an innocent animal as a representative picture of the substitutionary sacrifice of Christ, so that they could be restored to the relationship. He promised them of a coming one who would crush the head of the serpent. In their disobedience, they had lost righteousness. They needed righteousness. The animal skins were pictures of the perfect righteousness of Christ imputed to them. They didn't deserve that, but that is who He is. He did not have to do that for them or us, but that's what He did because He is full of grace (John 1:14). That's why the apostle Peter exhorted to, "rest your hope fully upon the grace that is to be brought to you at the revelation of Jesus Christ" (1 Pet. 1:13).

If anyone understood grace at this time of his life, it was Peter. He was the one that had the faith to get out of the boat but began to sink when he took his eyes off the Lord. He's the one that made the great proclamation that Jesus is the Christ and then immediately opposed the plan of God. And he is the one famous for denying the Lord three times before the rooster crowed. If anyone knew what the grace of our Lord was, Peter did. And he says to fix your hope fully on His grace, not on your works or your performance.

In his letter to Titus, the apostle Paul wrote, "For the grace of God that brings salvation has appeared to all men" (Titus 2:11). Paul was not an advocate of universal salvation. In other words, he did not believe everyone is saved because of Christ. What he does illustrate is that God's grace has extended undeserved favor to all people in that Christ's death and resurrection has placed all humanity into a savable position. Anyone can believe the gospel and get saved. "For God so loved the world, that He gave His only begotten Son, that *whoever believes* in Him should not perish but have everlasting life" (John 3:16, emphasis mine). His grace is extended to everyone, not just to a select few.

That's why he could write to Timothy that Jesus is "the Savior of all men, especially those who believe" (1 Tim. 4:10). The grace of God extends to everyone, including those who reject Him. Those who deny Him do not receive the benefit of the free gift of everlasting life offered to whosoever. They end up in the Lake of Fire not because they had no Savior, but because they rejected the one and only Savior, the Lord Jesus Christ.

Inevitably, at this point someone will raise the question, "What about the native in some far away land that never heard the gospel?" Typically this is often a way to deflect the decision that the person you are talking with needs to make about Christ. But the question also implies they believe there is a limit to the reach of the arm of God. Dikkie Ekiai writes in his personal testimony in a tract, *From the Jungle to Jesus,* how he came into a relationship with the Lord while growing up in the jungle in Borneo.[36] His journey began by observing the symmetry of a spider web that he saw one day in the jungle. He responded to the revelation about God according to the book of Romans, "What may be known of God is manifest in them for God has shown it to them" (Rom. 1:19). He responded to the light of God through the revelation in creation. The Lord gave him more spiritual light and delivered him from the tribal witchcraft and shamanism that he grew up in. He eventually came to the truth and believed on the Lord Jesus Christ. He states, "I was far from God and lived much of my life in total ignorance of the Christian gospel, but the Lord was able to reach me."[37] The grace of God can reach anyone anywhere.

Was not the Ethiopian eunuch saved similarly (Acts 8:26-38)? The Ethiopian had the word of God and was reading it when

---

[36]   Dikkie Ekiai. *From the Jungle to Jesus, Moments with the Book,* https://mwtb.org/products/pmt-from-the-jungle-to-jesus-at-peace-with-my-creator?variant=27602443847

[37]   Ibid.

returning to Egypt. He did not understand what he was reading though. He did not know of whom the Scripture (Old Testament) spoke. So God sent Philip to him, and he met the eunuch on his way home. Philip preached Jesus to him, and the eunuch understood the Scripture spoke of Jesus Christ. He believed and was baptized immediately. Philip did not know the eunuch was searching for truth, but the Lord knew. So he sent Philip to him to give him understanding. The grace of God can reach anyone anywhere.

Recently a friend of mine, who had been a missionary in Turkey, told me about a prisoner sitting in a cell reading the graffiti in a western Pennsylvania jail where he ministers. This man saw a small phrase etched on the wall, "Trust in God." That small simple statement spurred him on to seek the truth about God. He told my friend that seeing that caused him to pray to God for the first time in his life. They had an hour and a half conversation about the Lord because of it. The grace of God can reach anyone anywhere.

Several times we have had a booth at the local county fair. The fair lasts nine days so we would see and speak to a lot of people. One afternoon, a couple came strolling by. They had left home about an hour away and were heading to Falling Waters, a Frank Lloyd Wright landmark in Western Pennsylvania. In their journey, they had made some wrong turns and basically were lost. According to their testimony, they came up the road to the fair, not knowing it was there and were waved into the parking lot by a flagman. And so they decided to spend some time at the fair and forgot about going to Falling Waters. In doing so, they met us, and we spent an hour with them going through the gospel, helping them to see their spiritual need. The grace of God can reach anyone anywhere.

Just think about what you are doing right now that the Lord might be preparing for you. I remember when the Lord had gotten my total attention. I had been reading and studying the Bible. I started little by little. Then it became a half hour a day; then an hour a day. Then because of my job I could spend the whole morning day in and day out, reading, studying, writing things down. Finally, it came to a head. I had worked through feeling guilty about spending too much time being in the Scriptures. Yeah, that's crazy, but that's how spiritual warfare works. But then I knew I had to tell God that I was willing to go wherever He wanted to send me and to do whatever He wanted me to do. And with fear and trepidation, I told Him that. Was I going to Africa as a missionary? Did he want me to go into pastoral ministry? I had no clue. I had two young sons and lived on two beautiful acres in western Pennsylvania in the house my grandfather built. I didn't want to leave. We had recently moved back home to be close to family and friends. What would happen next?

I'll tell you what happened: nothing outwardly. I didn't move to another country, and I didn't change jobs. And I still live in the same house. God quietly began to use me right where I was. No thunder claps or lightning strikes. One day, a couple of years later, I realized God is looking for those who are available and are willing to be channels for His Word and His grace. By His grace, He prepared me for things that I had no clue that I would ever do. And by the way, He's never done with you until the day He calls you home. The grace of God can reach anyone anywhere. For you, it might be right in your own home.

Grace in the Old Testament

Another good question that some will ask is, "What about those in the Old Testament? How were they saved?" They were saved the same way: by faith in the substitutionary sacrifice of the Messiah. They looked forward to the cross. We look back to the cross.

I think they knew more than we give them credit. Jesus referred to Abel as the first prophet (Luke 11:50-51). Abel, son of Adam, brought a more excellent sacrifice than his brother because it was a lamb from his flock (Heb. 11:4; Gen. 4:2, 4). He knew God required a blood sacrifice that was a picture of the Messiah to come. Abel's faith was not in the lamb, but in the future "Lamb of God who takes away the sin of the world" (John 1:29).

All the prophets told of the suffering of Christ (Acts 3:18). The prophets said Christ would suffer and rise from the dead (Acts 26:22-23). They preached the same message from the beginning, pictured in the first sacrifice of the animal skins provided by the Lord and received by Adam and Eve. Job, the oldest book of the Bible, agrees the message was there; "For I know that my Redeemer lives, and He shall stand at last on the earth; and after my skin is destroyed, this I know, that in my flesh I shall see God" (Job 19:25-26).

The grace of God was right there communicating to them the truth of how man could be restored to the relationship with God. But the same thing that happened then happens today. Some received the truth and accepted the gracious offer of God by faith, and others rejected it.

The Grace of God in Sanctification

The grace of God not only saves us from the penalty of sin, but from the power of sin as well. Peter warned, "Beware lest you also fall from your own steadfastness, being led away by the error of the wicked, but grow in the grace and the knowledge of our Lord and Savior Jesus Christ" (2 Pet. 3:17-18). The grace that He extends to the world to save from the penalty of sin is instrumental in saving the believer from the power of sin; "teaching us that, denying ungodliness and worldly lusts, we should live soberly, righteously, and godly in the present age" (Titus 2:12). Some get concerned that teaching God's grace will lead to unrighteousness. But the opposite is true. Believers being transformed by grace will lead to godliness because grace teaches us to live righteously.

Understanding the grace of God is transformative. Jesus is the Word who became flesh. "And from the fullness of His grace we have all received, and grace for grace" (John 1:16). The idea is that Jesus gives us grace upon grace. It's unlimited! Apart from His grace, there would be no hope to live the Christian life. He displayed monumental grace through His substitutionary sacrifice on the cross. But His grace doesn't stop there.

As believers, He has also blessed us *"with every spiritual blessing in Christ"* (Eph. 1:3, emphasis mine). Because of His grace, we have a new identity and many undeserved spiritual blessings. These truths should transform your thinking about who you are in Christ:

1. We can know we have everlasting life that begins at the moment of faith (1 John 5:13).
2. We can know all of our sins have been forgiven (Col. 2:13).
3. In Christ, we are new creations (2 Cor. 5:17).
4. We are sealed by the Holy Spirit until the day of redemption (Eph. 1:13).
5. In Him, we have His perfect righteousness credited to us (2 Cor. 5:21).
6. We are children of God by faith in Jesus Christ (Gal. 3:26).
7. We can have fellowship with God through Christ (1 Cor. 1:9).
8. We can know God has a purpose for us as part of His eternal plan (Rom. 8:28).
9. We have peace with God (Rom. 5:1).
10. We can have the peace of God (Phil. 4:7-9).
11. We are now citizens of heaven (Phil. 3:20).
12. We have been brought near to God by the blood of Jesus Christ (Eph. 2:13).
13. We have been delivered from the power of darkness and conveyed into the kingdom of the Son of His love (Col. 1:13).
14. He has qualified us to be partakers of the divine inheritance of the saints (Col. 1:12).

15. We have an inheritance that is incorruptible, undefiled, that does not fade away, reserved in heaven (1 Pet. 1:4).
16. His divine power has given us all things that pertain to life and godliness (2 Pet. 1:3).
17. We are partakers of the divine nature (2 Pet. 1:4).
18. We have the hope of a resurrected glorified spiritual body, incorruptible (1 Cor. 15:42-44).
19. We are complete in Him (Col. 2:10).
20. We are partakers of the heavenly calling (Heb. 3:1).
21. We have been predestined to adoption as sons and daughters by Jesus Christ to Himself (Eph. 1:5).
22. We have the awesome privilege of being ambassadors for Christ and making disciples (2 Cor. 5:20; Matt. 28:19).
23. He provides for every necessity of life (Matt. 6:25-31).

In His grace, He has given us His Word. We started in the first chapter of this book speaking about the significance of His Word. It is only through His Word, the Bible, that we can begin to understand the grace of God. In His Word, He tells us about ourselves and how we got here. It's only through the Bible that we can know Him. We can understand some general revelation about Him through creation, but we never know how gracious and loving He is toward us until we understand His Word.

On that list are just some of the many spiritual blessings found in His Word that we have as believers in Jesus Christ. In His grace, He sends His Spirit to convict the world of sin, of righteousness, and of judgment. He then by His grace saves from the penalty of sin those who by faith receive the free gift of everlasting life. By His grace, He regenerates us, adopts us, and indwells us with His Spirit to deliver us from the power of sin so that we can live a purposeful, productive life that glorifies Him and is good for us.

The Lord did not have to give us any of the spiritual blessings needed to live life now. He could have saved us from the penalty of sin and then just made us wait to see what happens at the end of the road. But the Lord didn't. He gave us all these things and more in His Word so we can learn how to live a life now that honors Him and is good for us. And we can also know and have full assurance one day that we will also be saved from the very presence of sin! "Beloved now we are children of God; and it has not yet been revealed what we shall be, but we know that when He is revealed, we shall be like Him, for we shall see Him as He is" (1 John 3:2). Hallelujah! What a Savior! "For of Him and through Him and to Him are all things, to whom be glory forever. Amen" (Rom. 11:33).

In Conclusion

—◦⟶⟶◦◦⟸⟸◦—

The gospel is the most important message that God has given us. It is a simple message of how one can be restored to a relationship with God. But it gets muddled because of the way it is communicated. Often it is conveyed in a way that leads to doubt and fear, rather than assurance.

Just because a person can lack perseverance or falls away doesn't mean they were never saved to begin with. The possibility is always that one may not have understood the gospel and isn't saved. He or she may have thought walking an aisle, repenting of their sins, getting baptized, saying a prayer, or asking Jesus in their heart saved them from the penalty of sin. They may have placed their faith in something they did, rather than in the person and work of the Lord Jesus Christ. Or they may be blending justification and sanctification truths. So it is certainly wise to attempt to see what a person is trusting in. However, on the other hand, we cannot assume one is unsaved because he or she is not persevering or has fallen away from the faith.

For those who fall into serious sin, that is the purpose for church discipline, to restore them back to fellowship with the Lord. Why would the church, believers, be instructed to administer discipline, if we could not commit serious sins? But a child of God does not always respond appropriately to discipline. Sometimes they don't want to change, and so they leave. Such ones may never attend church again and may continue in their particular sinful practice.

Do we then write them off as "professing" believers and not "true"' believers, even if they understood the gospel and professed personal faith in Christ? I don't think God writes them off and we shouldn't either.

Believers who walk in darkness are still believers. They are out of fellowship with Him (1 John 1:6). They have sat down in the middle chair, living carnally. They don't have fellowship with God. The power of the sin nature can still be influential in the life of a believer. They can even be in a church and have actually fallen away from the faith, failing to persevere. They don't have to quit going to church to fall away.

We have already looked at the church at Laodicea (Rev. 3:14-20). Jesus was outside the church knocking, asking anyone in the church to invite Him in. If one did, he would come in and have a meal with him. Eating together in the Bible is a picture of fellowship. The church was in a relationship with the Lord, but they were out of fellowship with Him.

They thought they were wealthy and needed for nothing. But Jesus told them that they were "wretched, miserable, poor, blind, and naked" (Rev. 3:20). They had fallen out of fellowship with the Lord while still participating in church! They were walking in darkness, not in the light.

As a believer, it's important to understand one can fail miserably and go to heaven. Major failure in faithfulness may cause significant consequences. But getting to heaven, being delivered from the penalty of sin is not dependent upon you. It depends on the faithfulness of God.

However, being delivered from the power of sin does require faithfulness on the part of every individual believer. The purpose of the church is to preach the gospel and make disciples. We are in relationship with one another united by the Spirit of God in Christ to accomplish this ministry. If we are faithful to our calling, then believers will experience deliverance from the power of sin and bear fruit for God. We will become the functional and fruitful people God intended for us to be. This should be the desire of every individual in the body of Christ.

That's why grasping these truths from the Bible helps you and me to understand our position and condition. And the better one understands his or her position in Christ—that you are declared righteous, a child of God, adopted permanently into His family forever, unable to save yourself from sin's penalty, power, and presence—the more likely you will respond positively to His grace and lordship over your life. You will desire to live His way not because you have to, but because you want to.

You can dangle the possibility of hell over the head of a carnal believer to get them to straighten up. Doing that may even keep others in line so that their outward behavior is consistent with the standards of the law. That's what law does. It scares people or motivates people out of fear of penalty. It changes the person outwardly, but not inwardly. There's no transformation in that. Grace motivates people out of love for what the Lord has done. When a believer begins to cooperate with the Spirit of God, He begins to change you from the inside out.

When you realize nothing good dwells in you; that apart from Christ you can do nothing for God; that you can't live the Christian life; that it takes God to be godly; only then can you begin to grow in your relationship with God by faith (Rom. 7:18; John 15:5; Gal. 2:20). The old nature can never produce righteousness. Only the new nature can because it was created in true righteousness and holiness (Eph. 4:24).

This has been a major part of my journey, learning to understand these biblical truths about which I have written. I know grasping these things can make a difference in one's life because it made an enormous difference in my life. As I understood the grace of God more and more, the weights on my shoulders kept falling off. As a result, I started to live a "thank you" life rather than a "have to life."

My position in Christ could never change regardless of my performance. I came back to child-like faith, realizing we are delivered from the penalty of sin at the moment of faith alone in Christ alone.

Assurance of heaven can never be achieved by looking at one's performance. Those who teach that all "true" believers will persevere in faith, good works, and holiness, are misleading the flock. God desires believers to persevere, not grow weary, and not lose heart. Living faithfully requires perseverance, depending on the Spirit of God for the power. That's what we should do. But teaching that you will persevere, only makes you examine your outward behavior rather than looking to Jesus by faith. You can never live up to the perfection that the Lord requires. Your behavior, good or bad, will only create doubt or self-righteousness, and will never give one hundred percent assurance.

Assurance of heaven and living faithfully depends on taking God at His word, trusting in the promises and faithfulness of God. It made a world of difference for me. It can for you too.

Bibliography

Anderson, David R. *Bewitched the Rise of Neo-Galatianism*. USA: Grace Theology Press, 2015.

Ekiai Dikkie. "From the Jungle to Jesus at Peace with My Creator". Moments with the Book. https://mwtb.org/products/pmt-from-the-jungle-to-jesus-at-peace-with-my-creator?variant=27602443847.

Fleming, Jim. "Biblical Antiquity Center, Part 1," aired August 17, 2014, Christ in Prophecy, video, 19:00, https://christinprophecy.org/sermons/biblical-antiquity-center-part-1/.

MacArthur, John. *The MacArthur Study Bible*. Nashville London Vancouver Melbourne: Word Publishing, 1997.

McDonald, William. *Believer's Bible Commentary*. Nashville Atlanta London Vancouver: Thomas Nelson Publishers,1995.

Mikkelson, David. "Paul Harvey: 'If I Were the Devil' did radio commentator Paul Harvey pen an essay entitled 'If I Were the Devil'?" Snopes. (October 25, 2004). https://www.snopes.com/fact-check/if-i-were-the-devil/.

Onwubiko, Moses C. *James Faith without Works is dead*. Ontario: Essence Publishing, 2011.

Showers, Renald. *Spiritual Gifts*. Published by Renald Showers, 2007.

"The Trouble with Lordship Salvation." Presented in 1990 at Word of Life Annual Conference. http://www.middletownbi-blechurch.org/salvatio/lordsh10.htm.

Sproul, R.C. *Chosen by God*. Wheaton: Tyndale House Publishers, Inc. 1989.

Stegall, Tom. "Is 2 Corinthians 13:5 A Warning to False Professors?" *Grace Family Journal*. (July 3, 2018). https://www.gracegospel-press.org/is-2-corinthians-135-a-warning-to-false-professors/

Vine, W.E., Merrill F. Unger, William White Jr. *Vine's Complete Expository Dictionary of Old and New Testament Words*. Nashville Camden New York: Thomas Nelson Publishers, 1985.

Wilkins, Robert, Ed. *The Grace New Testament Commentary*. Denton: Grace Evangelical Society, 2010.